The Doubter's Novena

The Doubter's Novena
Nine Steps to Trust
with the Apostle Thomas

By Mike Aquilina and Christopher Bailey

With a foreword by Varkey Cardinal Vithayathil
Major Archbishop of the Syro-Malabar Church

Our Sunday Visitor Publishing Division
Our Sunday Visitor, Inc.
Huntington, Indiana 46750

WITH HIS GRACE 18 DEC 2013

In memory of June Estep Bailey

1925–2009

CONTENTS

FOREWORD

St. Thomas, one of the twelve apostles of Jesus Christ, is the founder of Christianity in India and is acclaimed as the Apostle of India.

Some historians have doubted the apostolate of St. Thomas in India, especially the traditions of his work in South India. But, following more recent studies, historians are more and more in agreement with the ancient and living tradition of the St. Thomas Christians of South India — that the apostle St. Thomas evangelized their forebears and founded Christian communities for them. The tomb of the apostle in Chennai and the testimony of several Fathers of the Church give greater support for this tradition. In his book *Eastern Christianity in India*, the great French scholar and member of the French Academy Eugene Cardinal Tisserant states that, considering the historical scholarship available today, we can firmly say there was an early apostolate of St. Thomas in South India. This has also been affirmed in the statements of recent popes, including those of Pope Benedict XVI. The Christian Church St. Thomas founded is now divided into different churches, both Catholic and Orthodox. Among these the Syro-Malabar Catholic Church is now one of the most vibrant missionary churches in the world.

The Doubter's Novena: Nine Steps to Trust with the Apostle Thomas, by Mike Aquilina and Christopher

Bailey, is unique. It is the result of a careful study of the traditions, both Indian and Western, about the apostle St. Thomas. The book brings out the apostle's deep personal love for Christ, simplicity of life, love for the poor, zeal in preaching the gospel, and his dying for it in faraway India.

St. Thomas's initial doubt about the resurrection of Christ ended in his firm faith in it with his proclamation: "My Lord and my God" (Jn 20:28). The authors of this book have written it in the form of a novena, with anecdotes from the life of the apostle as presented in the gospels and in various traditions. There is a prayer added at the end of each "day" of the novena. Those who read this book will be helped, just as Thomas was, to move from doubt to a total conviction that Jesus is our Lord and God.

— ✠ Varkey Cardinal Vithayathil
Major Archbishop of the Syro-Malabar Church

PREFACE

This is a novena for those who struggle — those of us who are skeptical by nature, or doubtful by disposition, or pessimistic by temperament — those of us who have a hard time working up the bubbling zeal of ordinary novenas.

"Doubting Thomas" can serve as a great patron for us. The Gospels tell of his movement from skepticism to trust. Tradition tells us how that trust was tested through the remainder of his earthly life, as he traveled to evangelize faraway India. Amid hardships, misunderstanding, and temptations, he prevailed — and he triumphed, with Christ — and he can help us to triumph, too. Thomas is honored in the Far East, and has won great favors through his intercession.

Each "day" of this novena begins with stories from the life of St. Thomas, drawn from the Gospels and the ancient traditions of the Church in India. Each story is followed by a brief meditation that applies the lessons of the apostle's life to our everyday lives today. Each day's reading ends with a prayer for God's blessing or the saint's intercession.

PROLOGUE

It was the darkest day of their lives. The Master was dead, and no doubt the authorities would be gleefully pursuing his followers now that the Sabbath was over. The disciples might very well share the Master's fate, crucified as rebel agitators. Crucifixion certainly worked as a deterrent: the fear of it had been enough to make Peter, who was supposed to be the leader now, deny his Master three times in the same night.

Now Judas the betrayer was gone, probably off to spend his blood money. Judas had always loved money, and you could buy a good piece of real estate for thirty pieces of silver. The eleven who were left expected to be surrounded by soldiers any moment now and hauled off for a show trial.

So ten of them locked themselves in the big room where they had spent their last evening with Jesus, cowering behind bolted doors, terrified that the Temple authorities would catch up with them.

Only one was missing. Thomas was out in the city somewhere, daring death to catch up with him.

And because Thomas was the only one of the group brave enough to show his face in public, he missed the best piece of good news the world has ever heard.

Day 1

The Idea of Thomas

All who ever lived still live.

So said John Henry Newman in summing up Christian belief about the immortality of the soul. Of the holy souls, the ancient creeds tell us something more: that they live in communion with us. "We believe in the communion of saints . . . and life everlasting." The afterlife is a non-negotiable article of faith for Christians. Everyone who ever drew breath on earth is still alive today.

Some individuals, however, live more public afterlives than others. No one can travel far in the world without encountering shrines and churches dedicated to the apostles Peter and Paul, or hymns raised to the Blessed Virgin Mary. Other saints — like Winifred in Wales, Charbel in Lebanon, Januarius in Naples — remain vividly present for a limited and local public.

And then there's Thomas, a saint at once universal and local in his cult. Tradition tells us that, after decades of preaching and wonderworking in India, he suffered martyrdom there around 72 A.D. His earthly life was rich in adventure, as he journeyed over land and sea, but his afterlife has been, in some ways, even more remarkable. Thomas has managed perhaps the most colorful and varied postmortem career in human history. Consider his recent resumé.

A book purportedly about his teaching — *Beyond Belief,* by Princeton scholar Elaine Pagels — spent more than a year and a half on the hardcover best-seller list of the *New York Times.* The apostle may have made the professor a millionaire.

Headlines in India proclaimed that Thomas not only foresaw the great tsunami of 2004, but set its limit on the land — and the tsunami obeyed. The Christians who had sought refuge on the far side of the "Thomas post" say that the apostle saved their lives.

In the rain forests of South and Central America, indigenous tribes — now, as they have done for more than four centuries — are celebrating Thomas as their special patron, claiming that he found his way to their shores almost a millennium and a half before Columbus sailed the ocean blue.

Thomas has lived a most public and lively afterlife. Celebrity, however, is a magnet for trouble; and this is as true for saints as it is for starlets. Thomas suffers from identity theft in some areas of the world, and from outright denial in others. For the Thomas who appears in the best-sellers bears little resemblance to the apostle whose memory Christian India reverently preserves. The Christians of India, for their part, have been far more cautious and conscientious about their history than the scribes of North America. Readers in the West should have the opportunity to see all the evidence for themselves, and to come to know the Thomas who lived and lives still.

For Thomas's *true* story has changed the Church and the world in significant ways — and not only because the phrase "doubting Thomas" has entered almost every earthly language. The biblical Thomas is best known as the doubter. But it was he who launched devotion to the Sacred Heart — arguably the most recognizably Catholic devotion in the world — when he cured his doubt by gazing upon Jesus' wounded side.

The apostle Thomas is living still. To that fact, the Scriptures give ample testimony. He lives because he is a saint, one of the "great cloud of witnesses" (Heb 12:1). He lives because, as an apostle, he is one of the "twelve foundations" of the heavenly Jerusalem (Rev 21:14). He lives because, as a white-robed martyr, he intercedes in heaven for those peoples he left behind on earth (Rev 6:9-11).

He lives also, and abundantly, in the memory of the Christians of India, in their oral tradition and ancient songs, and in their ritual memory, the distinctive liturgies of their land.

Miracles and History

When the 2004 tsunami devastated India's southern coasts, Christians of Kerala attributed their miraculous survival to the apostle's protection. An old story told how

St. Thomas drove a post into the ground and promised that the sea would never rise beyond it. Indian Christians point out an ancient post as the one Thomas left, and indeed the sea stopped there. A large crowd of believers, meanwhile, had gathered in safety on the far side of the post, in the Mar Thoma Cathedral, the world's most renowned church dedicated to St. Thomas.

Why would the Christians of Kerala believe such an unlikely story — and stake their survival on it?

They believed it because they believed they knew what sort of man Thomas is. The man who said, "Let us go also, that we may die with [Jesus]" (Jn 11:16) is just the sort who would drive a post into the ground and dare the sea to pass it.

The Thomas in John's Gospel is a vivid character, a man of flesh and blood with all the idiosyncrasies and quirks we expect in a real human being. Either John was a brilliant novelist, or he simply described a friend he actually knew — a friend with whom he shared the most intense experiences of his life.

In the Bible, Thomas has only a few lines to speak. But we'll find that just those few lines sharply define a personality. And when we go beyond Scripture to the ancient traditions of Thomas's life, we'll find that same sharply drawn personality. The Thomas of the legends, and the Thomas of current Indian devotion, is the same Thomas we know from John. He is the bold speaker who dares to say what everyone else is thinking. He is the fearless apostle who will follow the Master, even when it seems to mean certain death.

Miracles are almost by nature disputable, because they defy our notions of nature. We can legitimately doubt whether Thomas actually did intervene to protect his cathedral from a tsunami. It's a question of faith, and even faithful Christians can question it.

But the belief in these miracles is solid fact, an inescapable truth of sociology. Thousands of Indians really do believe that Thomas saved them from the tsunami. The water came; it spared the cathedral; Indian Christians saw a miracle, Thomas saving them from the wave. Those are all demonstrable facts, even if the miracle itself is not.

We've just made an observation of staggering importance for the study of history. When we read a saint's life or other account studded with unlikely-sounding miracles, we can't use the miracles as evidence against the historical accuracy of the account. The tsunami did come; the cathedral was spared. No matter how the Indian Christians interpret those events, they are real events, and surprising ones. We don't have a right to dismiss the facts simply because some observers believed they added up to a miracle.

Now, in the ancient world, every unusual event was a miracle. We might almost say, more simply, that every event was a miracle. For most people, nothing was outside the range of the supernatural powers, and a successful journey was as much a miracle as salvation from a great flood. If we read that Aeolus sent a favorable breeze, we may dismiss Aeolus as the superstition of an outmoded religion. But it doesn't follow that the wind never came. If we read that Egyptian magicians could turn a staff into a serpent, we may suspect sleight-of-hand rather than magic — but we have no reason to suppose that the trick was never performed, any more than we have to doubt the word of someone who says a magician pulled a quarter from behind his ear.

Miraculous healings and exorcisms are facts of everyday life. How many television preachers have made their fortunes by smacking the foreheads of the faithful to "heal" incurable diseases? How many hundreds are present to witness the supposed miracle, and how many millions more see it on television and believe? The event is a fact, and that it was interpreted as a miracle is also a fact. Whether it was indeed miraculous is still an open question, but — from the historian's point of view — almost an irrelevant question.

We've just found a key that opens up great treasures of history. When we hear accounts full of miracles, we can't simply dismiss the accounts because the miracles don't fit our scientific notions. It's a true historical fact that, for most of history, most people have believed in miracles.

Yet we do tend to dismiss those accounts, because our modern prejudices can't stomach the miraculous. That's a sad loss to truly scientific history.

When we see that all the traditions agree that Thomas went to India; that every ancient author puts him there; that the Christians of India have been telling visitors that their Church was founded by Thomas since time immemorial; and, finally, that the route from the Mediterranean to India was wide open and heavily traveled — when we see all these things, we should be inclined to give some weight to the story that Thomas went to India. It isn't a certainty, but the careful scientific historian must admit it as a strong probability.

What is the evidence?

First, there are the Western writers. Every single writer who deals with the later careers of the apostles places Thomas either in India or in Parthia. The distinction between India and Parthia was blurry: for example, Gundaphorus, a historical king who has a starring role in one version of the Thomas legend, was a Parthian who ruled a vast territory in India.

Second, there are the Eastern writers, who are equally unanimous. Earliest among them is the anonymous author of the *Acts of Thomas*, a long pseudo-biography with strong Gnostic flavoring that nevertheless seems to preserve some older tradition of the life of Thomas.

The witnesses to Thomas's apostolate in Parthia/India include some of the greatest of the early Church Fathers, writing in a variety of languages and from far-flung places: Pseudo-Clement; Origen of Alexandria; Eusebius of Caesarea; Rufinus of Aquileia; Socrates the historian; St. Ephrem of Syria; St. Gregory Nazianzen; St. Ambrose of Milan; St. Gaudentius; St. Jerome; St. Paulinus of Nola; St. Gregory of Tours; and many others.

Finally, there's the Indian oral tradition. Because we live in a society where printing and information storage are ubiquitous, we find it hard to imagine how information can be transmitted accurately without writing. But, in fact, in societies where there is indeed an oral tradition, that oral tradition is astonishingly good at preserving an account. In India, scholars have shown that oral tradition can preserve the important facts of a story for many centuries.

A Catholic should know better than most people the value of tradition. Yet Western Catholics are often quickest to dismiss the stories of Thomas in India.

We're not going to dwell very much on the evidence for and against Thomas' voyage to India. Historians would have to say it's not scientifically *certain* that Thomas made it to India. But the preponderance of evidence is in favor of placing Thomas in India. Given what we know, it's more reasonable to accept the traditions than to reject them.

Meanwhile, the *story* of Thomas is an indisputable historical fact. It's a story the Indian Christians have been telling for centuries — longer, in fact, than Christianity has been established in most of Western Europe. The story of Thomas inspires them, guides them, and shows them what it means to be a Christian. If we're willing to listen, learn, and pray, it can do the same for us.

Just like Thomas . . .

Just like Thomas, we live in a world where history has meaning. We struggle to make sense of it, and we're tempted to give up and say that current events have no meaning at all, that life itself is meaningless, that the universe has no meaning and no purpose.

But we'd be wrong to give up. Part of faith is believing that every life has a purpose: that's why life is so sacred to Christians. And we have to believe not only that other innocent lives have their purpose — which is easy because it's distant and abstract — but that our *own* lives have a purpose as well, even though we're so wrapped up in our own chaos and frenzy that we can't see the purpose right now.

Prayer

O Glorious apostle, St. Thomas, the Eternal Father filled you with special gifts while on earth; the Holy Spirit kindled your heart with the fire of love for Jesus. Impelled by this love and inspired by the gifts of the Holy Spirit, you sojourned to India and became a martyr for proclaiming the Name of Jesus and the good news of salvation.

We, too, have received the precious gift of the faith you proclaimed. So we ask you to make our hearts burn with the same love of Jesus and be filled with a thirst for making Him known to other people. Show us how we are to fulfill this duty of our Christian calling in our own walks of life, and may our entire life be according to the teaching of Christ.

We beseech you, O St. Thomas, to intercede for us poor sinners and to use your miraculous powers to heal the sick and the suffering and to help us to see the face of God in the people around us.

O St. Thomas, we implore you to pray for us and to bless us by stretching out your blessed hand that touched the Sacred wound of Jesus Christ and that is anointed by His Precious Blood, so that we may find enough strength to carry the cross and to follow Jesus till our death. Amen.

— Traditional Novena Prayer to St. Thomas

DAY 2

THE BLESSINGS AND BURDENS OF HISTORY

Thomas was born in a world strikingly like ours. It was a world just learning to deal with a global economy: one great superpower ruled the entire Mediterranean, and its trading tentacles reached as far as Britain, China, and Ethiopia. Ancient traditions fought to keep their integrity against the onslaught of modern ideas. And millions of people looked to ancient Eastern wisdom for answers to modern problems.

Scripture tells us nothing about the early life of Thomas, and even legend is silent. But we can deduce quite a bit from what we know of Jewish life in his time.

The name "Thomas" means "Twin," as does his Greek name, "Didymus." It seems that Thomas had a twin brother or sister, although history has forgotten this other "Thomas." In one tradition, his twin was a sister named Lydia. On the other hand, a curious legend circulated among the Gnostics — heretical sects that claimed secret knowledge of Christ's hidden teachings — that Thomas was the twin brother of Christ himself. The legend was probably suggested simply by the name "the Twin," but it proved useful to the Gnostics when they adopted Thomas as their fictional spokesman. It is probably true that he was about the same age as Jesus; most of the disciples were within a few years of Jesus' age.

Tradition tells us that his given name was Judas, or Judah — an extremely common name among Jews of the tribe of Judah. Two of Jesus' other disciples were also named Judas: Judas Thaddaeus, commonly known as St. Jude, and Judas Iscariot, who betrayed Jesus.

The Jews probably came closer to universal literacy than any other ancient people. Knowing the Law was every Jew's duty, and to know the Law one had to be able to read it. That meant learning to read Hebrew, although Aramaic — a related language — was now the everyday language in most of Palestine. It was also helpful or even necessary to know at least some Greek, the language of business throughout the eastern Roman Empire. Even a common tradesman's son might grow up trilingual, with at least some literacy in all three languages.

So Thomas probably grew up literate and well versed in the Scriptures, because that was how Jewish boys generally grew up in those days. We can see the results in the preaching of Jesus: even when he preached to the common rabble, Jesus assumed a high level of familiarity with Scripture. He amplified and interpreted the Law in the Sermon on the Mount, but he took it for granted that his audience already knew the Law.

Thomas would also have grown up with a trade, since there is no indication that his family was wealthy enough to be beyond the need of making a living. A Jewish boy would work at his father's trade as a sort of apprentice to his father, until the time came for him to take over the family business. In the Thomas legends, Thomas is a carpenter. If he was indeed a carpenter, he must have been brought up very much the same way Jesus was brought up. They would have shared many early experiences — which might also have contributed to the legend that he was Jesus' "twin," so alike were they.

As he grew up, Thomas would have visited Jerusalem frequently for the great festivals prescribed in the Law. Luke tells us that Jesus' parents went to Jerusalem every year for the Passover (Lk 2:41), even though Jerusalem was quite a walk from Nazareth. They traveled in a large group of relatives and friends. One year, when Jesus was twelve, they had come a day's journey out of Jerusalem before they noticed that Jesus was missing (Lk 2:44) — which shows how large the group of relatives and friends must have been. It also shows another aspect of Jewish village life: a boy like Thomas would have had practically the whole village as guardians. He would have been brought up not just by his parents, but also by his aunts and uncles and cousins and friends of cousins.

The constant communication with Jerusalem meant that news traveled quickly in the Jewish world. Not long after Jesus started drawing crowds with his teaching, the young man Thomas must have heard the rumors of him. Then, one day, he met the Master himself.

We have no account of that meeting. In the first three Gospels, Thomas appears only in the lists of the twelve disciples; in John's Gospel, we don't meet him until near the end of Jesus' ministry, when he had been following Jesus for a long time. But wherever the Gospels do tell us of Jesus' meeting with one of the disciples, we can see that there was something magnetic about Jesus. He called ordinary men who had plenty of ordinary work to do, but they dropped everything to follow him. They believed they had found the Anointed One, the Messiah — *Christ* in Greek — and from now on, the world would be very different.

It's clear that there were many different kinds of messianic expectation among the different sorts of Jews in Jesus' time. But there was definitely a popular image of the Messiah as a conquering hero, something like one of the heroes in the book of Judges: someone who would at once defeat Israel's enemies in battle and restore her right relationship with God. Would-be messiahs had already appeared more than once in recent history; usually they managed only to provoke a short riot before being squashed by the superior forces of the Romans. But one lasting result of their rebellions was that the Jewish authorities, desperate to keep a good relationship with their Roman overlords, were always on the lookout for the next troublemaker who declared himself the Messiah. The last thing they wanted was another messiah running around stirring up trouble.

The disciples were a diverse lot. They were mostly drawn from the lower classes, but we have to remember that the lower classes among the Jews were quite likely the best-educated lower classes in the world. The scribes might sneer at them as uneducated louts, but that was only relative to the many additional years of learning it took to become a lawyer.

- Simon Peter was a fisherman from Galilee. He knew the Law and was faithful to every letter of it. But he was an impulsive sort, prone to sudden decisions that he might regret later. Nevertheless, Jesus chose him as the leader of the Twelve, and Peter's career after the Ascension more than justified the choice.

- Andrew, Simon Peter's brother, was also a fisherman, and we can guess that his background was similar to Peter's. It was Andrew who first introduced Peter to Jesus; after meeting Jesus himself, he ran back to tell his brother, "We have found the Messiah!"

- James "the Great" — probably so called because he was physically bigger than James, son of Alphaeus — was one of two sons of Zebedee among the Twelve. He was probably a cousin of Jesus.

- John, Jesus' best friend, was the brother of James the Great. John had some sort of inside connections at the Temple: he was able to get himself and Peter admitted to the trial of Jesus. He was perhaps the closest thing to an "insider" among the Twelve. Mary, the mother of Jesus, lived with John after Jesus' crucifixion.

- Philip was another Galilean from the same village as Peter and Andrew. He was probably also a fisherman.

- Bartholomew (or Nathanael) is known in Scripture by one sarcastic remark — "Can anything good come from Nazareth?" — made when his friend Philip told him that the Messiah had been found. But he overcame his doubts, and one strong tradition says that he also ended his life in India.

- Matthew (or Levi) was a tax collector — an occupation that gave him a comfortable living but earned him the undying hatred of his neighbors. Some of the Jewish extremists insisted that it was forbidden for Jews to pay taxes to the Romans at all. But even those who accepted the principle hated the tax collector: as an independent contractor, his profit depended on collecting more money than he had to send to the Roman government, and the best way to get rich in the job was to bleed the people dry.

- James, son of Alphaeus — or James the Less — was Matthew's brother. He might also have been a tax collector, but we know nothing for certain about his background.

- Judas (or Thaddaeus), son of James, left only one sentence attributed to him in the Gospels, but his subsequent career would make him one of the most loved of all the saints.

- Simon "the Zealot" was one of those Jewish extremists who would have hated Matthew the tax collector. The Zealots were a terrorist movement who believed in expelling the Romans by force, or at least dying in the attempt.

- Judas Iscariot seems to have been a well-bred sort who knew something about money. Jesus and the rest of the disciples made him their treasurer; he kept the common purse and supervised expenditures. When no one was looking, he took a bit off the top for himself. He must also have been a deeply tortured soul: he betrayed Jesus for money, changed his mind and tried to give back the money, and — when that failed — hanged himself.

And then there was Thomas.

Only John among the Gospel writers tells us anything about what Thomas said or did, but the few things John tells us reveal quite a lot about the personality of Thomas.

The first mention of Thomas as an individual comes near the end of Jesus' public ministry. Jesus was, once again, on the run from angry mobs, having escaped across the Jordan when the Temple authorities tried to have him stoned.

In fact, it seems that Jesus was in hiding for a good bit of the last few months of his ministry. He came out for brief surprise appearances, then vanished again before the authorities could catch up with him.

Nevertheless, Jesus knew the game couldn't go on forever. When the news came that his friend Lazarus was very ill, Jesus stayed where he was for two days, safely across the Jordan and out of reach of the Temple authorities. Then, he shocked his disciples by saying, "Let us go back to Judea."

"Rabbi," they sputtered incredulously, "the Jews were just trying to stone you, and you want to go back there?" ("The Jews" meant the Temple authorities, as it usually does in John's Gospel.)

Jesus at first gave them an enigmatic reply.

"Are there not twelve hours in the day? If one walks during the day, he does not stumble, because he sees the light of this world. But if one walks at night, he stumbles, because the light is not in him."

Then he gave them a more direct explanation. "Our friend Lazarus is asleep, but I am going to awaken him."

He meant, of course, that Lazarus was dead, although his friends didn't understand him until he said so directly. "Lazarus has died. And I am glad for you that I was not there, that you may believe. Let us go to him."

So he really was set on going to Judea, and he really did expect them to go with him. The disciples must all have been thinking the same thing: "We're all going to die." But only Thomas dared to speak.

"Let us also go," he said to the rest, "so that we may die with him."[1]

This is the first time in Scripture that Thomas appears as anything more than a name. The Gospels are all very sparing in details. But the fact that John chose to introduce us to Thomas this way suggests that John — who was a careful literary craftsman — thought this little outburst said a lot about Thomas. Thomas has a small part in John's Gospel, but he will play a pivotal role at the climax of the book, so it was important for John to introduce his character well.

So here is the first thing we learn about the personality of Thomas: he possesses a peculiar combination of pessimism and dedication. He's sure they're all going to die, but he's determined to follow the Lord even so. The

---

[1] Jn 11:1-16 (verse 16 from NRSV).

Thomas story everyone remembers absolutely depends on that peculiarity of his character.

That memorable story is the story of his doubt — the story that made "doubting Thomas" a popular catch phrase. We seldom notice that it's also the story of his courage.

After Jesus was crucified, John tells us, the disciples were all cowering behind locked doors "for fear of the Jews" — the "Jews," once again, meaning the Temple authorities. There was no telling how far the authorities would go to stamp out the Jesus movement; with the Romans in a crucifying mood, it was wise to keep the doors locked.

It was while they were locked in a room together that Jesus appeared to them and "showed them his hands and his side" — which still bore the marks of his very real death on the cross.

But only ten of the Twelve were in the room. Judas the betrayer was gone, of course. And Thomas was out somewhere. While the rest cowered behind closed doors, Thomas was daring death to catch up with him. He was still willing to die for the Master.

Yet he refused to believe the others when they told him Jesus was alive. "Unless I see the mark of the nails in his hands and put my finger into the nailmarks and put my hand into his side," he told them defiantly, "I will not believe."

Still dedicated, and still a pessimist: Thomas was willing to die for the Master, even though he was positively certain that all was lost. He had the dedication it would take to be a true apostle of Christ. What he needed was a once-and-for-all cure for his despair.

A week later the disciples were once again gathered in the same room with the doors locked, and this time Thomas was with them. Again Jesus came. He greeted the whole group with "Peace be with you"; then, he turned straight to Thomas.

"Put your finger here and see my hands, and bring your hand and put it into my side, and do not be unbelieving, but believe."

Thomas had no need to try the experiment. His reply was instant: "My Lord and my God!"

"Have you come to believe because you have seen me?" Jesus asked. "Blessed are those who have not seen and have believed."

John makes perfect use of this story to bring home the truth of Jesus' death and resurrection. If scholars are right in supposing that the Gospel of John was written near the end of the first century, then there were already Gnostic sects springing up that denied the reality of Christ's death on the cross. Many denied the Incarnation entirely; they said that the Son of God only *seemed* to take on a human body. But in John, we see the scene through Thomas' eyes, and we too feel the overwhelming reality of the Resurrection. All his doubt was removed at once, in one powerfully vivid experience.

Pope St. Gregory the Great spoke of this in his homily on that passage:

Do you think this happened by chance, that one of the disciples was absent then? And that when he came later and heard the news, he doubted? And that, having doubted, he touched, and having touched, believed?

No, this didn't happen by chance. It was divine dispensation. God's mercy made it happen in a wonderful way, so that the doubting disciple, while he touched the wounds in his Master's flesh, should by doing so heal the wounds of our unbelief.

Thomas' unbelief means more to our faith than the faith of the disciples who believed. While he is brought back to faith by touching, our own minds are freed from doubt and built up in faith.

Just like Thomas . . .

Just like Thomas, we're plagued by doubt. It's human nature to be doubtful, and our skeptical society encourages us to doubt even more.

It's not just questions of religion, either. Look at the crazy conspiracy theories all over the Web. AIDS was created in the laboratory to wipe out half the population. Airplane contrails are really "chemtrails," poisons sprayed for some nefarious purpose by secret powers who control the whole aviation industry. The Queen of England is actually an evil lizard bent on enslaving the human population. These are things people seriously believe, because we're almost programmed to assume the worst.

Ironically, when we hear good news, we just can't believe it. If it's too good to be true — well, it must be a lie, mustn't it?

Yet, at the same time, we hate living in that world of doubt. What we yearn for more than anything else is certainty. We want to *know*. We want to *believe*. We want to have a strong faith.

Thomas the apostle has been speaking to our doubt quite a bit lately. Neo-Gnostics and other professional doubters have picked him as their spokesman, the one who doubted. Thomas refused to believe in the Resurrection, which is the very event that defines Christianity as more than a way of "being nice to each other."

But doubt is never an end in itself. What we've forgotten in our skeptical age is that doubt is a *means*. In fact, it's one of the essential steps toward certainty.

Without doubt, there could be no knowledge. No one would ever ask, "How do you *know* that?"

And this is the real story of Thomas in the Gospel. The doubt is the *beginning* of the story. The end is certainty: "My Lord and my God."

In fact, the story of Thomas has brought untold believers to Christ. Jesus used the doubt of Doubting Thomas not just to convince Thomas himself but to bring millions and billions of souls home to heaven. Including us, if we'll let him.

Just like Thomas, we have a hard time believing the Good News. But Christ is ready to use our doubt. Instead of leading us away from faith, our doubt will lead us straight to Christ — if we take it seriously.

God knows that we doubt. He built us that way, so that we would always be looking for the truth. If we're willing to be *real* skeptics, keeping our minds open and asking God for help in finding that truth, Christ will bring the truth to us. It may not be as dramatic as the scene in John's Gospel, but it will happen. Our doubt will lead us to Christ.

Prayer

O glorious Apostle Thomas, who led to Christ so many unbelieving nations: hear now the prayers of the faithful, who beg you to lead them to Jesus.

So that we may merit to appear in his divine presence, we need, before all other graces, the light which leads to him. That light is Faith; then, pray that we may have faith.

Our Savior had compassion on your weakness, and deigned to remove from you the doubt of his having risen from the grave; pray to him for us, that he will mercifully come to our assistance, and make himself felt by our hearts.

We do not ask, O holy Apostle, to see him with the eyes of our body, but with those of our faith, for he said to you, when he showed himself to you, "Blessed are they who have not seen, and have believed!" Of this happy number we desire to be.

We beseech you, therefore, pray that we may obtain the Faith of the heart and will, so that we also may cry out, "My Lord and my God!"

— Adapted from Greek liturgical prayers
(See *The Liturgical Year* by Dom Prosper Guéranger,
prayers for December 21.)

DAY 3

LESS THAN PERFECT

After the Resurrection, Jesus spent forty days teaching his disciples about the Kingdom, preparing them for their own missions. Many other people besides the Twelve also saw him: Paul tells us that, at one point, the risen Lord appeared to more than 500 people. We have no other record of that appearance, and Paul's offhand reference leaves us panting for more details. The irony is that Paul's reference is so offhand precisely because his original hearers knew all about the incident: Paul reminds them that they can just go out and ask one of the 500 about it, since most of them are still alive.

The Gospels and the Acts of the Apostles give us only a few snapshots of Jesus' life between the Resurrection and the Ascension. We don't have enough information to make a complete post-Resurrection biography of Jesus, and we don't know specifically what he taught his disciples during that time. We can tell from the stories in the Gospels that he didn't spend the whole time with them; rather, he appeared to them occasionally, first in Jerusalem and then back in Galilee.

But we do know that he had a very specific mission in mind for them: "Go into all the world, and preach the gospel to the whole creation" (Mk 16:15).

The very last words in Matthew's Gospel are what Christians call the Great Commission.

> And Jesus came and said to them, "All authority in heaven and on earth has been given to me. Go therefore and make disciples of all nations, baptizing them in the name of the Father and of the Son and of the Holy Spirit, and teaching them to obey everything that I have commanded you. And remember, I am with you always, to the close of the age."

> — Mt 28:18-20

The mission was clear: the disciples were to go to every nation on earth.

"But you will receive power when the Holy Spirit has come upon you," Jesus promises them in Acts 1:8; "and you will be my witnesses in Jerusalem and in all Judea and Samaria and to the end of the earth."

The fact that the same commandment appears so many times in the New Testament, in various forms and at various times, shows that the first Christians considered it one of the primary principles of their religion. They took it seriously; Jesus had really meant them to go to all nations. But how were they going to do that?

The Acts of the Apostles tells us quite a bit about what happened to Peter, but it tells us little to nothing about the acts of the rest of the Twelve after the scene leaves Jerusalem. Ancient tradition, however, tells us that the apostles did go to all nations, following Jesus' commandment.

According to several of the ancient stories, the apostles chose their destinations by lot. There was certainly precedent for casting lots to make an important choice: that was how the eleven remaining disciples had chosen a successor to replace Judas Iscariot. Faced with two equally qualified candidates, they prayed for guidance, and then tossed a coin. The method makes perfect sense if you believe that God directs the outcome of the toss.

We can imagine the solemn quiet as, one by one, the old friends drew their lots. We can imagine each of them saying a silent prayer. And we can imagine the look of horror on his face when Thomas drew his lot and discovered that his prayer had apparently not been answered.

Here's how the *Acts of Thomas*, a book that probably dates from the 200s, tells the story:

> When the apostles drew lots, Judas Thomas, the Twin, drew India. But he didn't want to go; he was too weak to travel, he said. "I'm a Hebrew. How can I go to the Indians and preach the truth?"
>
> While he kept arguing that way, the Savior appeared to him at night and said, "Don't be

afraid, Thomas. Go to India and preach the Word there, for my grace is with you."

But he refused. He said, "Send me anywhere you like — as long as it's somewhere else. I won't go to India."

Just like Thomas . . .

Just like Thomas, we're less than perfect. We're fearful, timid, uncertain, and lazy. We're angry, ill tempered, resentful, and judgmental.

We hardly deserve to be called Christians! After all, if we were really Christian, we'd be following the teachings in the Sermon on the Mount, wouldn't we?

But do we turn the other cheek? Do we go two miles when someone grabs us by the collar and orders us to go one? Do we bless those who curse us?

Probably not. Even if we try very hard, we can't always live up to the standard Jesus sets for us. And most of us don't try as hard as we should.

So how can we bring the good news to others if we can't live up to the Gospel standards ourselves? Shouldn't we wait until we've mastered the Christian life ourselves before we start trying to make converts?

The answer is in the Gospels, and in the book of Acts, and in the stories of Thomas.

Jesus chose twelve ordinary men, not twelve extraordinarily well-behaved ascetics, to be his apostles.

The New Testament is full of stories about just how ordinary they were. Judas Iscariot betrayed Jesus for money, but he was only the worst case among a dozen backsliders and sinners. Peter denied Christ three times, and hardly missed an opportunity to make the wrong decision. Bartholomew couldn't believe that anything good could come from Nazareth. James and John greedily scrambled for top positions in the coming Kingdom. Paul "opposed" Peter "to his face" over the Gentile question (Gal 2:11).

And Thomas was afraid to go to India.

But these were the men Jesus charged with bringing the good news to all nations. How on earth could they possibly do it?

Jesus didn't threaten them. He didn't tell them, "You'd better shape up, or I'll get myself a dozen good apostles." Instead, he did what a good teacher always does: he promised them help, and he kept his promise.

What Thomas learned on his way to India, and what all the other apostles learned in their own missions, was that you can't wait until you're perfect yourself. That will never happen. But if you plunge forward anyway, Jesus has promised that the Holy Spirit will be with you every step of the way.

On the other hand, if you hold back because you're afraid you're not good enough, you're not the kind of faithful servant Jesus hoped you'd be. Jesus told us a story to show us how we'll be judged on how we used God's gifts:

For it will be as when a man going on a journey called his servants and entrusted to them his property; to one he gave five talents, to another two, to another one, to each according to his ability. Then he went away. He who had received the five talents went at once and traded with them; and he made five talents more. So also, he who had the two talents made two talents more. But he who had received the one talent went and dug in the ground and hid his master's money.

Now after a long time the master of those servants came and settled accounts with them. And he who had received the five talents came forward, bringing five talents more, saying, "Master, you delivered to me five talents; here I have made five talents more."

His master said to him, "Well done, good and faithful servant; you have been faithful over a little, I will set you over much; enter into the joy of your master."

And he also who had the two talents came forward, saying, "Master, you delivered to me two talents; here I have made two talents more."

His master said to him, "Well done, good and faithful servant; you have been faithful over a little, I will set you over much; enter into the joy of your master."

He also who had received the one talent came forward, saying, "Master, I knew you to be a hard man, reaping where you did not sow, and gathering where you did not winnow; so I was afraid, and I went and hid your talent in the ground. Here you have what is yours."

But his master answered him, "You wicked and slothful servant! You knew that I reap where I have not sowed, and gather where I have not winnowed? Then you ought to have invested my money with the bankers, and at my coming I should have received what was my own with interest. So take the talent from him, and give it to him who has the ten talents."

— Mt 25:14

God has given us abundant gifts. That's true of every one of us, no matter how much we doubt our own abilities. Where we fail, God steps in to help. What we lack, God fills in.

So will we use those gifts and bring God back more than he invested in us? Or will we hide them away and try to forget about them because we don't think we're good enough?

Thomas nearly gave up before he made it to India — that's what the stories say. But he didn't give up completely. Jesus was there to help him through his doubt yet again.

He's still here to help us through our doubt, but we have to be willing to ask for the help. We have to be willing to do what he asks of us, even if we're not perfect.

Just remember that the apostles weren't perfect, either. But if you look at the two billion Christians in the world today, you can see what they accomplished.

Prayer

Lord Jesus, Saint Thomas doubted your resurrection until he touched your wounds. After Pentecost, you called him to become a missionary in India, but he doubted again and said no. He changed his mind only after being taken into slavery by a merchant who happened to be going to India. Once he was cured of his doubt, you freed him and he began the work you had called him to do. I ask him, as the patron saint against doubt, to pray for me when I question the direction in which you are leading me. Forgive me for mistrusting You, Lord, and help me to grow from the experience. Saint Thomas, pray for me. Amen.

— Traditional Prayer to St. Thomas, Patron of India

DAY 4

WHAT THE WORLD KNOWS

India! What a long way away that was, and what strange stories Thomas must have heard about the place! No wonder he refused to go.

Yet India was no mere myth in the Mediterranean world. Every Mediterranean harbor was filled with the scent of Indian spices. Every wealthy lady showed off her Indian pearls and fine gowns made from Indian muslin. Even much of the everyday clothing that ordinary people wore was made with Indian cloth. And, of course, there was pepper — vast barns full of it on the Tiber in Rome, and huge stocks in every other city in the Empire. The cooking of the Empire absolutely depended on pepper; it was not a luxury but a necessity.

At the height of Rome's trade with the east, more than 120 ships a year sailed from the Mediterranean to India, by one modern historian's estimate. Pliny, a Roman writer who lived at about the same time as Thomas, complained that Rome was spending a hundred million sesterces a year on Indian goods — "That's how expensive our luxuries and our women are." You don't even have to know what sesterces are to know that that's a lot of them. (To put the figure in perspective, at that time a Roman soldier was paid 900 sesterces a year, so a hundred million sesterces would have been enough to pay an army of more than a hundred thousand men.) Many of those Roman coins still turn up in India, especially in the southern part. Classical Tamil literature confirms that the Indian ports were filled with foreigners from the West, speaking strange languages.

Trade went the other way, too. Indian merchants were common sights on the streets of Alexandria in Egypt, and Roman goods came into India in enormous quantities.

So India was far from unknown; many hundreds of people made the trip there and back every year, and in the sailing season ships departed for India at a rate of more than one a day.

Why, then, do all the traditional stories portray Thomas as utterly dismayed to learn that he would be sent to India? The answer may be that it was not the experiences of merchants and sailors that defined India for him, but rather the fables and exaggerations of popular legend.

Classical writers on India present us with little more than tall tales. If we had only Pliny to go on, for example, we'd be forced to conclude that India was a mythical country about which the Mediterranean world knew nothing. (Keep in mind as you read the following that Pliny was renowned in his day as a scientist and a naturalist.)

On a certain mountain called Milus, there are men whose feet grow backward, and on each foot they have eight toes, as Megasthenes reports.

And in many other hills of that country, there is a kind of men with heads like dogs, who wear skins of wild animals. They bark instead of speaking, and they are well armed with sharp claws. They live on the prey they get by hunting wild animals and birds. Ctesias writes that more than 120,000 of them were known to exist.

Ctesias also reports that in a certain part of India the women bear only once in their lives, and the babies grow old and gray as soon as they are born into the world.

There is also a kind of people named Monoscelli, who have only one leg apiece; but they are very nimble, and hop with great speed. These people are also called Sciopodes, because in the hottest part of the summer, they lie on their backs and shade themselves from the heat of the sun with their feet. Ctesias says that these people are not far from Troglodytes.

And again, farther west from these, there are some who have no heads on their necks, but carry their eyes in their shoulders….

In the farthest eastern part of India, near the source of the Ganges, there is a nation called the Astomes, because they have no mouths. They have hair all over their bodies, but they wear clothes of the finest cotton and down that come from the leaves of trees. They live only by the air, and by smelling sweet odors, which they draw in through the nose. They take no food or drink: only pleasant smells from various roots, flowers, and wild fruits growing in the woods. They take those things with them whenever they go on a long journey, so that they will have something to smell. And yet if the scent is anything strong and foul, they are soon overcome by it, and die.

—Adapted from *Natural History*, Book 7

Of course, to be fair to Pliny, some of the amazing reports of India were not exaggerated. "Under one fig tree, believe it or not, whole squadrons of horsemen may stand, kept covered and shaded by the branches." That is literally true: whole villages even today are built in the shade of a single banyan tree, which is indeed a species of fig.

Still, most of his information is obviously myth and fable. All of it is drawn from other writers, not from the experience of any of Pliny's contemporaries who had been to India. If more than a hundred ships a year made the trip to India, why couldn't Pliny simply talk to someone who had seen the place?

The answer is that it would never have occurred to him. A respectable fellow like Pliny talking to a common sailor? How absurd!

Strabo the geographer had the same problem trying to find accurate information about India, and he admitted it quite frankly:

> But we should take what we hear about this country with a grain of salt. For not only is it very far away from us, but not many of us have seen it. And even the ones who have seen it have only seen bits and pieces of it, and most of what they say comes from hearsay. Even what they did see, they learned while marching through the country quickly with an army. So they don't give us the same stories about the same things, even though they wrote those stories as if what they said had been checked thoroughly.

Once again, we might ask, why didn't he talk to one of the merchants or sailors who had seen India? Strabo anticipated that question, and he gave an answer that any upper-class reader (which is to say anyone with the leisure to read his book) would have understood:

> As for the merchants who sail to India these days by way of the Nile and the Arabian Gulf, only a few have gone as far as the Ganges. [The Ganges is in the eastern part of India, far from the usual trading ports frequented by Mediterranean ships.] And those are mere

> private citizens, so they're useless as far as the
> history of the places they've seen is concerned.

Merchants and sailors go to India all the time; but they're "private citizens," so their information is useless. It boils down to a question of class: a sailor, no matter how much firsthand experience he had, simply wasn't a respectable source of information. It was useless to talk to merchants and sailors, because they moved in the wrong circles. They wouldn't find out anything worthwhile about India. So, no matter how much one distrusted the written accounts of India, one had to rely on the respectable writers who had dealt with the subject.

We see the same problem over and over in every kind of classical writing. Tacitus — an unusually careful historian — repeats the most absurd and insulting rumors about the origin and history of the Jews. When Tacitus was writing, there were thousands of Jews in Rome. Any one of those Jews could have given him the Jews' own version of their history. But it never occurred to him to ask. Instead, he took his information from respectable sources — namely, other Latin and Greek writers who would no more think of speaking to a Jew than Tacitus would.

Pliny likewise took his stories from reputable sources, some going back to the time of Alexander. That their information was 400 years old only made it that much more respectable. These were books that had been in circulation for quite a long time: they were recognized classics. Anyone who read Pliny would have known that he had chosen his sources well.

What Pliny shows us is that there were some wild stories about India circulating in the Mediterranean world. It's likely that those stories — not the actual experiences of sailors and merchants — would have been the things Thomas heard about India. And, of course, there's no guarantee that he would have got any accurate information from sailors, even if he had talked to them. We can easily imagine a slightly inebriated mariner winking to his fellow sailors as he spun out fantastic tales of Indian adventure for the benefit of an increasingly wide-eyed landlubber.

Just like Thomas . . .

Just like Thomas, we fear the unknown. It's natural and human to fear what we don't understand. But sometimes God challenges us to plunge ahead and do his work, even when we don't know what we're getting into. He may not call us to the ends of the known world, but we make our own alien worlds right here. We draw invisible lines through our own neighborhoods that we're afraid to cross.

Here's an example: in our culture these days, there's often a wide gulf between the suburbs and the city. That's especially true when the suburbs are settled primarily by one race and the city by another.

Many suburbanites are afraid to go into the city — afraid they'll be robbed, or murdered, or just laughed at.

Many city-dwellers are afraid to go into the suburbs, for almost exactly the same reasons. We're afraid to go where the people are different from us. We hear crazy stories about those places, just like the crazy stories Thomas heard about India. Aren't they all redneck bigots in the suburbs, who form lynch mobs at the drop of a hat? Aren't they all drug dealers with machine guns in the city, who like to use suburbanites for target practice?

The wisdom of the world tells us to listen to those crazy stories. *Stay out of those neighborhoods*, our friends warn us. *Stay here where it's safe, where everyone is like you.*

But sometimes God has different ideas. *Go help the people who lost their houses in the wildfire*, he tells us. *Go teach the children whose parents have to toil all day at backbreaking jobs just to make the rent payment. Take my message to people who look different from you*, God tells us: *on the inside, they look just like me.*

Is God calling us to martyrdom, like Thomas? Probably not right now. Even Thomas, who went to far-off India, lived longer than most of the apostles who stayed in the comfortable old Roman Empire. We all have to die some day, though, and God is calling us to a life that will prepare us to leave this life joyfully and enter the greater life he has waiting for us.

What God is asking us for is a bit of trust — trust in God, first of all, and trust in the people made in his image. When we push our limits and go out into the world, we find that there are good people everywhere waiting for us, hungry for the message we have to bring them. They welcome us and make us feel at home, even on the other side of our invisible line. We learn to see the image of God in them, and so we learn a little bit more about what God looks like. We've learned a little about crossing lines between worlds, which helps us prepare just a little bit more for that last crossing we're all going to have to make.

Prayer

Grant, O Lord, we beseech you, that we may always have the assistance of the prayers of your blessed apostle Thomas, and zealously profess the faith he taught. We pay, O Lord, the homage due to you, humbly beseeching you to preserve us in your own gifts. Assist us, O merciful God, and grant our prayer, by the intercession of blessed Thomas the apostle, to preserve in us, what you have bestowed upon us.

— Adapted from a nineteenth-century missal,
translated by Bishop John England

Day 5

MOUNTAINS AND OCEANS

What we do know about India in classical Roman times doesn't come from classical writers. We've already seen how disdainful they were of the people who'd actually been there to see the place for themselves. Mere private citizens weren't suitable company for a respectable writer.

But while the best classical writers were repeating the most absurd rumors and tall tales, the businessmen who hoped to get rich on the trade were busy shuffling back and forth to India as fast as their ships would carry them. And by a curious coincidence — we might almost say a providential coincidence — their ships had started to carry them much faster just about the time Thomas would have been going to India.

Trade with India had been important for a long time even before the Romans conquered the whole Mediterranean world. Greek merchants had long settled in the southwest of India; as early as about 500 B.C., we find Indian inscriptions that mention "Ionians" ("Yavana," which was the local way of pronouncing the word "Ionian"). They came in ships laden with gold and wine, their most valuable commodities. They left with the one thing that was more valuable to them than either: black pepper.

In 326 B.C., Alexander the Great, having already wiped out the Persian Empire, turned his attention to India. In a few months, he had conquered and subdued the area around the Indus. His soldiers refused to go farther, but Alexander already held the greatest empire the world had ever known. It was an empire of empires, stretching from Greece to India, and taking in Palestine, Egypt, and Persia along the way.

Three years after he added India to his Empire, Alexander died in Babylon. The empire did not survive him; it broke into various squabbling chunks ruled by different generals. Together, though, these chunks covered nearly the whole area Alexander had conquered, and they were ruled by Greek-speaking emperors.

In India, a large Greek-speaking population remained, and although borders were constantly shifting, it was necessary even for rulers who were not Greek themselves to have their important edicts translated into Greek.

It's hard to overestimate the effect Alexander's adventures had on the world around him. But for our purposes, it's enough to point out that a merchant could go from Greece to India by land without ever having to learn a new language. Everywhere he went would be people who spoke Greek. The travel itself might be difficult, depending on who was at war with whom, but Greek was now the universal language of trade from the Mediterranean to the Indus.

If you were a merchant hoping to strike it rich in the Indian trade, there were two ways to get to India: by land and by sea. Both were hard journeys at first.

The famous Silk Road brought the luxuries of the East to Rome — spices from India and silk from China. In the other direction, it took the luxuries of the Mediterranean world eastward, especially gold and wine.

Few merchants traveled the whole length of the Silk Road. Instead, goods moved a bit at a time through a long series of transactions. A merchant would carry silks westward and trade them for other merchandise; the buyer would take the silks a bit farther west and sell them at a higher price; and so on till they reached the upper classes in Rome, by which time they had been marked up half a dozen times.

Pepper and other spices could travel the same route from India — and, again, the cost was enormously inflated by intermediate profits.

Besides, while the silk route got you to India, it was a long and arduous journey over land that was almost as hostile as the people who lived on it. And any little shift in the balance of power among any of the clans and tribes along the way might shut off the route indefinitely. Then where would the silk come from? What would happen to the pepper?

So the sea was a very attractive option. But there again, the sea routes were under the control of intermediaries who might or might not be friendly to the Roman merchants. Arab traders sailed to India and bought the spices, silks, and luxuries the Romans craved; then, they came back and sold them to Roman traders for a hefty profit. At any time, they might get annoyed about something, and then the sea route was cut off.

Imagine how the economy of the United States would suffer if trade with the East — Middle to Far — suddenly stopped, and the flow of oil, cheap electronic goods, and flimsy plastic doodads were cut off all at once. It would be a catastrophe, and we're willing to do quite a bit to make sure it doesn't happen.

The same was true of the Romans. Obviously, it would be much better to be in control of the trade route to India than to rely on intermediaries.

The first step was conquering Arabia, or at least enough of it to gain control of the useful ports. Under Augustus, the Romans took control of the Arabian coast, opening it all up to Roman merchants.

But India was still a long distance away. Considering the amount of sea they controlled, the Romans were not very adventurous sailors. Their normal practice was to hug the shore all the way, never letting the land out of their sight. Following the land from Arabia to India meant taking a long arch-shaped course, with detours into every bay and inlet. Roman ships took the best advantage they could of the route, trading at every stop. But it took a long time to get to India and a long time to get back, and that made Indian goods expensive.

A sort of traveler's guide called the *Periplus of the Erythraean Sea* tells us what could be found at every port, what the natives were like, what they had to sell, and what they wanted to buy, for the whole jagged route.

But then, it tells us of a remarkable discovery:

> Now, they used to make the entire voyage from Cana and Eudaemon Arabia, just as we've described it, in little vessels that sailed close to the shores of the bays. Hippalus was the pilot who, having observed where the ports were and what the seas were like, first discovered how to plot a course straight across the ocean. For when the Etesian winds are blowing for us, the wind is coming in off the ocean on the shores of India. This southwest wind is called the Hippalus, named after the man who first discovered the route across the sea.

This man Hippalus belongs in the list of great nautical adventurers, right up there with Leif Ericsson, Columbus, and Magellan. Doubtless terrifying his crew, he boldly left the land behind and trusted that his deductions were correct. And he was right.

Suddenly, the main part of the voyage was shorter by months. Ships could go to India and come back in the same year, bringing the wealth of India back with them and making Roman investors rich. Hundreds of ships made the trip every season.

A scrap of paper called the Vienna Papyrus tells us quite a lot about that Indian trade. This document is a loan agreement between two Greek merchants: one lives in Muziris, India's chief port for the Roman trade, and the other in Alexandria. We learn that importers had to pay stiff taxes on Indian goods, but it was obviously still a very profitable business. The mere fact that merchants from the Roman Empire had permanently settled in India tells us how attractive the profit was. We also know that the merchants were in constant touch with Alexandria — they had to be, so they could know what goods were worth sending that way.

So there were people in India who made it their business to keep track of everything that was going on in the Roman Empire, and there were people in the Roman Empire who made it their business to keep track of India in the same way. Far from being isolated worlds, India and Rome were bound together by unbreakable ties of profit and gossip. Whatever was going on in Alexandria, it didn't take long for the news to reach India.

There were also Jews in India, and every tradition tells us that Thomas — like the other apostles — brought the Good News to them first.

We don't know how long the Jews have been in India. Their own traditions say that the Jews of Kerala have been trading with India since Solomon's time. Whether they formed a substantial community or not, it's almost certain that there were Jews in India as soon as there were Greek and Roman trading colonies there. Jewish merchants were some of the most daring and enterprising traders in the Mediterranean world. It's hard to imagine that their keen eye for profitable trade and their hardy spirit of adventure wouldn't have drawn them to the fabulous wealth of India. Thus, when the legends tell us that Thomas found Jewish communities already in India, we have no reason to doubt them and every reason to believe them.

So we see that the real India was very different from the India Thomas would probably have imagined. Thomas would have heard the wild stories of barbarians and monsters, and he would have imagined that it was next to impossible to get to India, or to survive among the monsters if he did get there. However, in fact, God seems to have been working for more than five centuries to make it easy for Thomas to get there. It was almost as if God had been doing for Thomas what he did for the Israelites in the Exodus, drying up the sea and making a path where there had been none before. Everything was providentially arranged: Thomas could join any of the hundreds or thousands of travelers who made the trip every year, and he could get along in Greek the whole way. If Thomas could just trust in Christ, he would soon discover that all his fears were groundless.

Just like Thomas . . .

Just like Thomas, we have a hard time trusting in God's providence. Yes, we know what Jesus said about sparrows. "Are not five sparrows sold for two pennies? And not one of them is forgotten before God. Why, even the hairs of your head are all numbered. Fear not; you are of more value than many sparrows" (Lk 12:6-7). But it takes some effort for us to believe that in our hearts, even if we nod approvingly when we hear it read in church.

There's nothing wrong with being careful. When Satan tried to persuade Jesus to jump off a skyscraper (the Temple was certainly a skyscraper by first-century standards), he quoted from Psalm 91:

> For he will give his angels charge of you
> > to guard you in all your ways.
> On their hands they will bear you up,
> > lest you dash your foot against a stone.

But Jesus answered from Deuteronomy 6:16: "You shall not put the Lord your God to the test."

So Jesus doesn't ask us to be foolish or careless. But he does ask us to do what we know is right, even when it's hard or potentially dangerous. And he asks us to trust in the help he promised us.

Consider what God told Jeremiah when Jeremiah was called to be a prophet:

> "Before I formed you in the womb I knew you,
> and before you were born I consecrated you;
> I appointed you a prophet to the nations."

Now, Jeremiah didn't ask to be a prophet. He didn't know how to be a prophet, and he was sure he wouldn't be any good at it.

> Then I said, "Ah, Lord GOD! Behold, I do not
> know how to speak, for I am only a youth."

But Jeremiah was missing the point. God was asking him to do something beyond his capabilities — that was perfectly true. But Jeremiah would not have to rely on his own capabilities.

> But the Lord said to me, "Do not say, 'I am only a youth';
>> for to all to whom I send you you shall go,
> and whatever I command you you shall speak.
> Be not afraid of them,
>> for I am with you to deliver you, says the Lord."
> Then the Lord put forth his hand and touched my mouth;
>> and the Lord said to me,
>> "Behold, I have put my words in your mouth.
> See, I have set you this day over nations and over kingdoms,
>> to pluck up and to break down,
> to destroy and to overthrow,
>> to build and to plant."

> — Jer 1:5-10

God knew from the beginning who Jeremiah was, and God had chosen a mission for him — not just for anyone but for Jeremiah in particular. And no matter how inadequate Jeremiah feels (and it's absolutely true that he is inadequate by himself), God will be there to give him what he needs for his mission.

This is the way God calls every one of us. He has known us all since before the beginning of creation. He knows what we can do, because he made us with those abilities. He knows when we need help. And he won't ask us to do anything we can't do — as long as we remember to accept the help he offers us.

That's what makes trust so essential. But understanding it also makes trust a little easier. We can't possibly know what lies ahead, because we can't see the future. But God sees the future, the past, and the present all at once. When we realize that God isn't in the dark the way we are, it's a little easier for us to accept that God knows what he's doing.

Prayer

Almighty and ever-living God, who strengthened your apostle Thomas with sure and certain faith in your Son's resurrection: Grant us so perfectly and without doubt to believe in Jesus Christ, our Lord and our God, that our faith may never be found wanting in your sight; through him who lives and reigns with you and the Holy Spirit, one God, now and for ever.

— Traditional liturgical prayer
(Quoted by the Rev. John T. Mathew in *Christian Light of Life*, May 2006.)

Day 6

Spice and Silk

We left Thomas refusing to go to India, even when Christ himself promised him grace. But at that moment, according to the legend in the *Acts of Thomas*, an Indian merchant showed up looking for a carpenter.

We have to be careful about the *Acts of Thomas*. In the form in which it's come down to us, it's full of Gnostic influence. The Gnostics were a heretical group, or a cluster of heretical groups, who believed that only they knew what Christ really taught ("Gnostic" comes from the Greek word for "knowing"). The Christian doctrines taught by the Catholic Church were for the ignorant and unenlightened; the few who had been chosen knew the real truth. The real truth usually turned out to be a bunch of mumbo-jumbo sayings laced with polysyllabic philosophical terms, something like Yoda dictating fortune cookies. Nevertheless, the idea of "secret wisdom," revealed to you and your friends exclusively, is always very attractive. It makes the real Gospel, which is out there for anyone to see, seem common and vulgar.

So we have to be careful about the Gnostic influence. On the other hand, the *Acts of Thomas* preserves some genuine historical knowledge. The Indian king in the story is Gundaphorus. In the heady days of nineteenth-century rationalist scholarship, the whole book was assumed to be a "novel," completely fictional, and no king named Gundaphorus was known to Western history. But then, rather inconveniently, his coins began turning up in northwestern India. Today, we know a good bit more about the history of that area, and we're forced to admit that there really was a king by that name. Score one for the *Acts of Thomas*.

What seems likely is that the *Acts of Thomas* preserves the outline of a traditional story of Thomas' later career, along with an overlay of Gnostic philosophy that isn't really part of the story. This traditional outline is also the outline of the traditional Thomas stories in India, and it fits with the meager scraps of information other early writers give us about what happened to Thomas. So that brings us right back to the Indian merchant who was looking for a carpenter.

> And while Thomas was still refusing to go to India, it happened that a certain merchant named Abbanes came from India, sent by King Gundaphorus. The king had commanded this merchant to buy a carpenter and bring him back to India.

> When the Lord saw Abbanes walking in the market at noon, he said to him, "Are you looking for a carpenter to buy?"

And Abbanes said to him, "Yes, I am."

"And the Lord said to him, "I have a slave who's a carpenter, and I'm hoping to sell him." And saying that, he pointed to Thomas, who was some distance away. So they agreed that Abbanes should pay three pounds of silver, and the Lord wrote a deed of sale:

> I, Jesus, son of Joseph the carpenter,
> acknowledge that I have sold my slave by the
>   name of Judas
> to you, Abbanes, a merchant of Gundaphorus,
>   king of India.

And when the deed was finished, the Savior brought Judas Thomas to the merchant. When Abbanes saw him, he said, "Is this your master?"

And the apostle said, "Yes, this is my Lord."

Abbanes said, "I've just bought you from him."

And the apostle was silent.

The next day the apostle got up early, and having prayed to the Lord, he said, "I will go wherever you wish, Lord Jesus. Your will be done."

So he went with Abbanes the merchant, taking nothing with him but the price Abbanes had paid for him. For the Lord had given him that, saying, "Take your price with you, along with my grace, wherever you go."

Thus Thomas sets out on his great adventure. He's had to give up the comforts of home — which probably weren't very comfortable, since he was by no means a rich man. But they were familiar comforts, and familiarity is the most comfortable thing of all.

But he soon finds a different sort of comfort. Arriving in India, Thomas ends up at a wedding feast where the wine flows like water and the food is the best that can be procured. There's also a beautiful young woman, a flute player, who seems quite taken with him.

> The flute-girl, carrying her flute with her, went from one man to the next and played for everyone. But when she came to the apostle, she stood over him and played right beside him for quite a while, because she was also a Hebrew by nationality. . . .
>
> She left him to play for the rest of the guests, but she kept gazing back toward him. She was happy to see him, because he was one of her own nation; but he was also the best-looking man at the banquet. And when she had finished playing to the rest of the guests, she sat down next to him, gazing at him earnestly.

It's possible that "flute-girl" is a bit euphemistic here. It was common in ancient feasts to provide all forms of entertainment. Women who could play music might well be hired prostitutes, assigned to serve the guests as a favor from the host.

At any rate, Thomas is surrounded by pleasures here, and he has a beautiful woman beside him who obviously adores him. It would be easy for him to just forget about his larger mission and indulge in every pleasure.

But he doesn't. He doesn't get drunk like everyone else, and he ignores the flute-girl's obvious advances.

Is it because pleasure is bad for Christians? No, of course not. Pleasure is good, but it can't distract us from what's most important.

This is an important and subtle distinction. We need to understand the difference between prudish abstinence and Christian temperance.

Wine, for example, is one of the good things on God's earth.

> Thou dost cause the grass to grow for the cattle,
>> and plants for man to cultivate,
> that he may bring forth food from the earth,
>> and wine to gladden the heart of man,
> oil to make his face shine,
>> and bread to strengthen man's heart.
>
> — Ps 104:14-15

But the Bible is also full of admonitions against drunkenness. People who are drunk do things that will make them miserable sooner or later. Wine brings joy; too much wine brings misery.

We have a choice to make: do we choose happiness or misery?

Sometimes it's a harder choice than we think. It doesn't depend on our circumstances, which often enough we can't control. It depends on what we do with our circumstances.

Although Thomas is denying himself fleeting pleasures in the story, he's choosing happiness over misery.

What gives him the power to see so clearly?

In one word, sacraments. The reality of Jesus Christ is made present and real for us in the sacraments — above all, in the Eucharist. When we keep our minds focused on Christ, we can see past the fleeting pleasure and pain of this world and into the unending bliss that waits for us. When we eat the bread and drink the wine, we share in the nature of Christ — not just metaphorically or abstractly, but in a real and concrete way. We become part of his body; his blood flows in us, too.

That's why the sacraments are prominent all through the Thomas stories, even though Thomas spends much of his life away from the rest of the Christian community. It's why the Indian Christians are so devoted to the sacraments today. Living for almost 2,000 years as a minority in their native land, they draw on the power of the sacramental life to give them the strength to go on.

Just like Thomas . . .

Just like Thomas, we have a choice before us. We can be happy or miserable — wherever we are.

What's the difference between a comedy and a tragedy? Not the events, but the way you tell the story. Specifically, it usually depends on where you end your story.

A comedy traditionally ends happily, and a tragedy usually ends miserably. The difference is not in the events themselves, but in where those events come in the story. The author of a tragedy usually ends his story when his hero is dead. The author of a comedy usually ends his story when his hero is happy.

All human beings die eventually. Does that mean all life is tragedy?

Only if we see death as miserable. But death is another circumstance of life, another opportunity for choosing happiness or misery.

We can believe what we've always said we believe about death — in which case death is a blessing, an end to the sufferings and imperfections of this life and a gateway to perfect joy. Or we can approach death with fear and doubt, in which case death is a misery. Death doesn't care which way we choose. It's coming whether we like it or not.

It really is true that choosing joy is always within our power. We have to remind ourselves of that constantly, because our circumstances won't always be pleasant. Every one of us will lose people we love; every one of us will suffer plenty of torments before the world is through with us. Yet we can still choose joy.

And that's the decision that faces us. Will we accept the joy Christ offers us? Will we choose happiness over misery?

It's easy when we put it that way. But it's not always so easy in practice. We have to remember the example of Thomas in the story. He had good food, good wine, and a beautiful woman right in front of him — but he stayed away from all of them. Why? Not because food or wine is bad in itself, and not because there's anything wrong with human love. Quite the reverse: those are great gifts that God has given us for our delight.

But we have to know when pleasure leads us away from real joy rather than toward it. We have to remember the goal. If we're too much attached to our little earthly pleasures, we'll miss the real joy that's waiting for us at the end of the road.

Prayer

Almighty Father, as we give honor to Thomas the apostle, let us always know the help of his prayers. May we have eternal life through our belief in Jesus, whom Thomas acknowledged as Lord and God.

— Traditional liturgical prayer, adapted
from the Sacramentary

◌◌◌

FLATTERY AND SUCCESS

The story tells us now that Thomas reached India, and Abbanes the merchant brought him to King Gundaphorus.

"Can you build me a palace?" the king asked.

"I certainly can," Thomas answered. "I can build it and furnish it; this is the work I came to do."

So the king took him out to examine the site, and asked him when he could get started.

"Not right now," said Thomas. "This isn't a suitable time. I can start this winter."

This was strange news to the king, and it probably made him a bit suspicious. "Everyone else builds in the summer," he said to Thomas. "Are you telling me that you can build a palace in the winter?"

"Yes," Thomas answered, "that's how it will have to be."

"Well, draw me a plan of this palace, so I can see that you really know what you're talking about."

So Thomas sat down and drew a magnificent plan, with everything indicated in exquisite detail right down to a supply of running water. Everything had been thought out with an eye equally to beauty and to practicality.

When he saw this drawing, the king's doubts vanished completely. "You are a true craftsman," said the king. "It's beneath your dignity to be serving kings."

This is the peak of success as far as the world is concerned. Thomas is designing a palace for a king. The only way he could be more honored is if he were the king himself.

So far the story is going just about the way we expect it, and we expect it to end up with a satisfied customer and everyone acknowledging that Thomas has built a truly magnificent palace. But that's not what actually happens.

The story tells us that the king had to go away for quite some time, but he promised Thomas that he would send all the money necessary for the construction. And he did go away, and Thomas did receive the money. But he didn't spend it on construction.

Instead, every cent Thomas received went to the poor and the sick.

After a while, the king sent a message asking, "What more do you need to finish the palace?"

Thomas answered, "The whole thing is built except the roof."

So the king sent him more money to finish the roof. Meanwhile, Thomas continued to give everything away. He taught the Good News everywhere he went; he healed the sick; he cast out demons. He kept himself very busy — but he wasn't building any palace, as far as the people around him could see.

Eventually the king came back, of course. As he entered the city, he started to ask his friends, "So what do you think of my new palace?"

"We haven't seen any palace," his friends answered him. "As far as we know, that architect of yours hasn't built a thing. He's given everything away to the poor, and he goes about healing people and casting out demons. Frankly, we think he must be some kind of sorcerer."

King Gundaphorus must have been more than a bit displeased already, but his friends went on. "Yet the good he does shows he must be a righteous man. He never keeps anything for himself. He eats nothing but bread and a bit of salt, and he wears the same clothes all the time. He gives away everything he has, and he doesn't take anything from anybody. Maybe he really is an apostle of that new God he keeps telling us about."

After hearing this news, the story says, King Gundaphorus sat shaking his head for a long time.

Finally he sent for Thomas and Abbanes.

"Have you built me the palace?" he demanded of Thomas.

"Yes, I have," Thomas answered.

"Well, when can we see it?"

"You can't see it now," Thomas said. "But when you depart this life, then you can see it."

Well, as you can imagine, the king was furious. He threw Thomas in prison, and Abbanes with him. Abbanes wasn't happy, but Thomas encouraged him. "Believe in the God I've told you about," he said, "and even if you lose this life, you'll have joy in the next life."

Meanwhile, the king was thinking what he should do with the two prisoners. Should he burn them? Flay them alive? How about both?

But the king's brother Gad took it even harder than Gundaphorus. He was so overcome with fury and vexation that, while he was in the middle of inventing new tortures for his brother to put the Jewish sorcerer through, he fell sick and died. The grief-stricken king, who had loved his brother dearly, ordered that the body should be prepared for burial with the greatest pomp.

In the meantime the angels took charge of Gad's soul, and they conducted him straight up to heaven. There he saw a palace more magnificent than anything he could ever have imagined.

"I beg you, my lords," he said to the angels, "let me live just in one of the littlest rooms of this palace!"

"That palace is not for you," the angels explained. "This is the palace that Thomas the Christian has built for your brother."

"Then I beg you, lords, let me go back to my brother! He doesn't understand about the palace — I know he'll sell it to me."

So the angels let his soul go, and just as the grave clothes were being put on the body, Gad sprang up from the bed and asked to speak with his brother.

King Gundaphorus was overjoyed when he heard that his brother was alive. He ran to see him with a crowd of followers.

As soon as Gundaphorus was beside him, his brother said very earnestly, "I know you would have given half your kingdom to me if I had asked for it, so swear to me that you'll sell me what I ask of you."

The king swore he'd give him any of his possessions.

"Sell me your palace in the heavens," said Gad.

"Now, where would I get a palace in the heavens?" Gundaphorus asked.

"I mean the one that Christian built for you — the Hebrew slave you threw in prison."

Then suddenly Gundaphorus understood. He knew that the palace represented the eternal bliss that would come through the faith that Thomas was teaching.

"I can't sell you that palace," the king told his brother. "But the man is still alive. He'll build you a better one!"

And Gundaphorus immediately had Thomas and Abbanes brought out of prison. Falling on his knees, he begged Thomas to pray that God would forgive him.

So Gundaphorus and his brother were baptized, and many of Gundaphorus' subjects were baptized with him. From a slave in prison about to be tortured to death, Thomas had suddenly risen to be the most honored man in the kingdom.

St. Ephrem the Syrian, who was familiar with some form of the Thomas legend, praised the apostle's supernatural skill in architecture in one of his poems. No one else in history, Ephrem says, ever drew up plans for a palace on earth and built it in heaven. We adapt two stanzas here in English verse:

> The Only Son of God twelve men did mark,
> Among them Thomas, whom he later sent
> To baptize people wandering in the dark:
> Into benighted India he went.
> When Thomas dawned, like morning's early light,
> He banished from the land the shades of night.
>
> Who else in history was ever known
> To raise in heaven what he drew on earth?
> No one but Thomas ever has been shown
> To have a mind of such exalted worth
> That here the bold designs that he sets down
> Should win in heaven an eternal crown.

Just like Thomas . . .

Just like Thomas, we have to balance earthly needs with heavenly needs. We need to remember what's really important, even when it's hard for us to look that far forward.

It's easy for us to let the earthly needs take over. We have families to support. We have people depending on us at work. The government wants its taxes. The supermarket seems to want an outrageous amount of money for a simple loaf of bread. The price of gas leaps from intolerable to outrageous. The transit authority says it has to raise fares again.

All those demands mean we have to work hard just to scrape by. There just isn't room to think of the distant future when the present is pressing in on us from all sides.

Yet the present, no matter how pressing, is transitory. It will be gone in a moment — the blink of an eye in cosmic terms. The future, after we die, lasts forever.

So how do we use the tools we have on earth to build ourselves a palace in heaven?

While we go about our earthly work, we should always be thinking of the palace we're building for ourselves in heaven. And here we can follow the example of Thomas in the story, and learn the lesson he taught Gundaphorus.

Look how Thomas went about building the palace for the king.

First, he took care of the poor and suffering. "Truly, I say to you, as you did it to one of the least of these my brethren, you did it to me" (Mt 25:40).

Then, he proclaimed Christ to the people. They had already seen his deeds, so they were more disposed to hear his words.

When the people were ready, he introduced them to the sacraments, baptizing them into the one, holy, catholic, and apostolic Church.

Finally, he was willing to give up his life for the faith. That didn't actually happen this time, but he was ready.

What King Gundaphorus learned from Thomas was that a palace on earth is worthless weighed against a palace in heaven. And you don't build your heavenly palace by piling up stones: you build it by living a Christian life and spreading the light to others.

But we want that earthly palace, don't we? We focus so much on our earthly success, or the lack of it, that we make it the only thing. And that attachment, that inability to set aside earthly things, leads us away from God. When God doesn't give us the earthly things we want, we grumble. When God allows us to suffer some inconvenience, we doubt. How could a good God allow suffering? How could a loving God let us die? How could a God who really cares not give us a million dollars? If there really were a God, would he treat us like this?

These are questions we can ask only because we don't see the real picture. We want to be in control of our own destinies, when what we really need for happiness is to give up control to God. When we run into obstacles, we blame God — but we should be thanking him. Those obstacles are our chance to learn what's really important. When we think we lack something we need, that's our chance to learn we don't need it. In the end — and the end is coming sooner than we think — the only thing that matters is that palace we're building in heaven.

Prayer

Saint Thomas, once you were slow to believe that the Lord had risen in glory. But later, because you had seen him, you exclaimed, "My Lord and my God!" Ancient tradition tells us you gave powerful assistance in building a Church where the pagan priests opposed it. Bless all architects, builders, and carpenters, that their work may honor the Lord.

— Traditional prayer to St. Thomas

Day 8

OPPOSITION AND DEFEAT

Once he was established as the king's favorite, things went very smoothly for Thomas. Indian tradition counts seven churches as founded by Thomas himself — and it's notable that six out of those seven were in cities where we know there was a substantial Jewish community in ancient times. It seems that Thomas followed the common Christian pattern of preaching to the Jewish community first, then moving outward to the Gentiles.

One distinctive feature of Thomas' evangelization, according to the tradition, was his use of the cross as a symbol of Christianity. Everywhere he founded a church, he set up a cross, and indeed the people of Kerala still point to certain ancient crosses as the ones Thomas set up, or at least the successors to his crosses.

Now, that doesn't strike us as all that strange, since we see the cross everywhere. But in fact the cross wasn't a common symbol in the West in the first generations of Christianity. Christians were more likely to use a fish as their symbol — or an anchor, which is a symbol of hope, though its resemblance to a cross may have been part of its attraction.

But tradition is very strong that Thomas adopted the cross right away. There's some evidence to support the tradition, too. In the middle 300s, a Christian known as Thomas of Cana arrived in India, where he found people who called themselves Christians. Thomas of Cana believed that these people had forgotten many basic principles and needed instruction in the faith, but he reported that they wore wooden crosses to distinguish themselves as Christians.

If the tradition is true, it seems wonderfully appropriate. Thomas was the apostle who refused to believe until he saw Jesus in front of him with the physical marks of the crucifixion on his body. The climax of John's Gospel is Thomas' declaration, "My Lord and my God" — an acknowledgment that the crucifixion was a real event, that Jesus Christ really died on the cross and rose from the dead. The message of Thomas is the physical reality of the crucifixion and resurrection of Jesus. Nothing could be more appropriate, then, than that Thomas should adopt the cross as the symbol of his faith, his absolute certainty, that Christ died and rose again.

The Indian tradition tells us of hundreds of miracles, and many thousands of converts baptized. Everywhere the faith was spreading.

But now the story takes a darker turn. We'll tell it the Indian way, since this is the way most of the Christians in the churches Thomas founded remember it.

The priests of the old order, the Indian stories say, could not look at the spread of Christianity without jealousy. As Thomas was traveling, the priests of Kali, whose cult was popular in that region, saw him passing their temple. They took the opportunity to waylay him. When they had surrounded him, they demanded that he bow down and worship the goddess. "That's the rule," they said. "No one gets by this temple today without worshipping the goddess. And if you do it right now, we'll give you some nice porridge to eat. Then you can get up and go, and no one will bother you anymore."

"Do you suppose I would worship Satan for a meal of unstewed rice?" Thomas replied. "I will never bow down to Kali. If I did bow down, this whole temple would be destroyed by fire."

"Oh really?" the priests sneered. "We've got to see that!"

Well, they asked for it. Thomas turned toward the statue of Kali and commanded the temple to catch fire. Instantly a blaze broke out, and the crowd fled in all directions. The statue of Kali leapt off its pedestal and ran away.

But in the confusion and terror, one of the fleeing priests grasped a lance and thrust it deep into Thomas' chest.

After that, they all fled, leaving Thomas to die alone in the woods.

But angels carried the news to Bishop Paulos, one of the faithful converts whom Thomas had appointed to oversee the new church in India. Paulos told the king, and they and a crowd of attendants rode like the wind to the site.

There, they found Thomas still alive. Having extracted the lance, Paulos tried to get Thomas into his chariot to take him back for healing.

"I don't need healing," Thomas told him. "My bliss is near."

After some last exhortations to his followers, Thomas died, and the angels carried his soul to heaven. His body was laid in the church, and for ten days the people mourned him.

Then suddenly a golden light shone from heaven. The people looked up and saw a palace, more beautiful than anything anyone had ever seen before. In the palace, on a throne, sat Thomas in magnificent state. He blessed all the people, and told them to remember his martyrdom. "Good will come to my children through me if they remember my death. I shall do good to all those who worship at my tomb."

Then the vision was gone. All the people went away to their houses. Their mourning had turned to joy.

Just like Thomas . . .

Just like Thomas, we're on a journey that ends in death. We ignore that inconvenient truth as much as we can, but in the end we'll have to face it.

We're all going to die. If jealous priests don't run us through with spears, then heart disease or cancer will do the job just as thoroughly. Or an accident, or a war, or an epidemic, or just old age.

It takes courage to be a martyr — to stand against opposition, knowing that the opposition might kill you. But perhaps even more, it takes a clearheaded realism. We know that death is inevitable; the martyr refuses to look away from that truth, but rather looks it in the eye. If death is coming anyway, then let it mean something, says the martyr. Let my death be a witness to God's love and power.

That's what the word martyr means: it's just the Greek word for witness. A martyr is someone who demonstrates the faith to the world.

These days not many of us are called to die for the faith in a spectacular way. We will all be called to die for our faith, though, and we need to remember that. The way we live needs to be a visible expression of our faith, and so does the way we die. Instead of being murdered by jealous pagans with spears, we're more likely to die in a hospital surrounded by beeping machinery. That, too, is a martyrdom, a witnessing, if we show the world how well a Christian can die.

But we shouldn't think that we couldn't possibly have to face dying for our faith the way Thomas did. It may be unlikely, but it could happen anywhere, at any time.

No one in democratic Weimar Germany could have predicted that in a few years, Nazis would be rounding up priests and sending them to die in concentration camps. It was just too unbelievable to imagine.

No one in thoroughly Orthodox Russia could have predicted that in a few years, Stalin would be sending priests off to Siberia to die in the salt mines. Who would have thought it?

No one in Catholic Spain could have predicted the bloodbath of the Spanish Civil War, when priests and consecrated virgins were slaughtered indiscriminately by leftists, driving the survivors into the scarcely more welcoming arms of the Fascists.

These were not Third-world backwaters. These were all civilized and highly developed countries, with long and proud religious traditions. And these things didn't happen long ago in the misty past, when people were primitive; in every case, there are still people living today who remember the horrors.

India today is also a civilized nation, with ancient and proud religious traditions and a long-established democracy that guarantees freedom for all. Yet there are thousands of Christians there today who suffer persecution, and sometimes martyrdom, because they are Christians. It's a big place, of course; in some Indian states, Christians are regularly persecuted, probably with the collusion of local authorities; in other states, Christians are themselves members of the establishment; and in still others, Christians are the majority.

In Kerala, where the legends say Thomas made his last stand, the Christians are still a minority, but largely prosperous. As long as anyone can remember, they have always had good relations with their more numerous

Hindu and Muslim neighbors. Yet even there, where Christians have been comfortable members of the establishment for centuries, they know they could still suffer for their faith. If the ancient and honored Hindu and Islamic traditions of tolerance and cooperation gave way to the new brands of fanaticism that have infected other parts of the country, the prosperous tropical paradise of Kerala could quickly become a war zone.

Yet the Christian faith endures, as it has done through two millennia of peace and war, conquest and independence. It endures as something distinctly Indian, as distinctly Indian as a Hindu temple or a kriti in classical Carnatic music. Yet it is just as much distinctly Catholic, and the Malabar rite, with all its exotic sounds, sights, and scents, is as Christian as a Mass in a Western suburban parish church with an electronic organ and a paperback missal.

Over all the proud and ancient spectacle of Indian Christianity stands the towering figure of St. Thomas, the founder of the Indian church, and still its apostolic guide — just as he promised he would be.

Prayer

O glorious Apostle Thomas, who led to Christ so many unbelieving nations: Pray, O holy Apostle, for the nations you evangelized, but which have fallen back again into the shades of death. May the day soon come, when the Sun of Justice will once more shine upon them. Bless the efforts of those apostolic men, who have devoted their labors and their very lives to the work of the missions; pray that the days of darkness may be shortened, and that the countries which were watered by your blood may at length see that Kingdom of God established among them, which you preached to them, and for which we wait.

— Adapted from Greek liturgical prayers
(See *The Liturgical Year* by Dom Prosper Guéranger, prayers for December 21.)

DAY 9

TRUSTING GOD

Now, at last, we've seen the whole career of Thomas, from doubt to trust, from timorous reluctance to joyful acceptance.

Like all of us, Thomas had plenty of flaws to begin with. He was a gloomy pessimist. John's Gospel shows him as the first to say, "We're all going to die," and the only one who refused to believe the good news of the Resurrection until he saw it for himself.

A lot of us are gloomy pessimists like that. Probably more so than in Thomas' own time: we live in an age of pessimism, where it's quite out of fashion to be cheerful.

Now, a pop psychologist might tell us that we have to get rid of that pessimism. And if it's just a pose, the pop psychologist is probably right.

But look what happened to Thomas. The stories of him in India show that he never really lost his character. Instead, the Lord refined it and turned it to good use.

As St. Gregory the Great pointed out, Thomas' doubt has been a greater blessing to the dubious than all the faith of all the believing apostles. His doubt led him to certainty, the blessed certainty that Jesus Christ is Lord and God.

Yet he was still the same gloomy pessimist, if we judge by the traditional stories. He was still tortured by the same kind of doubt. Yes, he knew for a fact that Jesus Christ had died and that he rose again, but did he really believe that Jesus would take care of him in India?

Still, Jesus demanded his trust, and circumstances beyond Thomas' control took over. Soon enough he was on his way to India in spite of himself.

There, he founded a church that still flourishes today, and there, he found the strength to face martyrdom with peace and joy.

Was he a changed man? Did he lose that pessimism that had plagued him earlier in his life?

Perhaps not. There's a flip side to Thomas' pessimism — the flip side we first saw in his very first appearance in John's Gospel. "He's going to die," Thomas told the other disciples when Jesus set out for Jerusalem. "We might as well go die with him."

The pessimism of Thomas sees that everything on earth is transitory. Nothing is reliable. If you have good things now, you might lose them tomorrow. The only thing worth clinging to is Jesus Christ.

It takes only one addition to turn that pessimism into optimism. The mature Thomas — the Thomas who cheerfully faced martyrdom in India — says the same thing: everything on earth is transitory, and it will probably be taken away tomorrow. But he makes one crucial addition: And so what?

That crucial difference marks the boundary between pessimism and detachment. Detachment is a good thing. You can enjoy the gifts God has given you, knowing that they might be taken away tomorrow; and instead of making you miserable, that knowledge only brings you closer to God.

What makes the difference is the certainty that Christ is the only reliable thing, coupled with the certainty that Christ is the only thing really worth having.

Then every setback brings us closer to Christ, because every setback helps us understand that the things of this earth are temporary. We can't have them forever. And if we have to lose them sometime, now is as good a time as any.

That's when we discover that we really can do it. Whatever Christ asks of us, we can give it a shot. What's the worst that could happen? We could lose our jobs? our homes? our lives?

Just like Thomas . . .

Just like Thomas, we don't think we can do it. Whatever Christ is asking of us, it's too much. We're not giants of faith like the apostles. Peter, Paul, Thomas — giants were on the earth in those days.

But they didn't look like giants to the people around them. They looked like men in way over their heads, the unlikeliest choices you can imagine for the founders of a Church.

Think how unimposing these great apostles were to the people who actually knew them.

Peter was a fisherman from Galilee. He sounded like a hick when he talked; the urban sophisticates from Jerusalem recognized his accent right away. It wasn't the sort of accent you expected to hear great ideas expressed in. Besides, he was wishy-washy, a known waffler who would take one side of a debate and then come round to the other side a few weeks later. He was also impulsive, prone to doing things he'd bitterly regret even just a few minutes afterward. *This* was the leader of the Christian Church?

Paul was well educated, but he was just a tradesman. He was a tentmaker. If you wanted to know about broad expanses of fabric, he was your man. But would you have thought of going to him for answers to the deeper questions of philosophy? Besides, he was short and bald and probably a bit hunched over; his looks didn't stand out at all in a crowd. He was also notoriously short-tempered and hard to get along with. *This* was the founder of Christian theology?

And then there was Thomas. In a religion that demands faith, he got the epithet "Doubting" stuck in front of his name forever. If we believe the ancient traditions, he was a carpenter like Jesus. Perhaps we'd call him more a general contractor these days: someone you'd call on to put up a building, but not someone you'd call on for a religious debate. He didn't believe a thing unless you showed it to him. He was pessimistic and reluctant, and he invented all sorts of excuses. He was sure he wasn't up to the job. *This* was the founder of the Church in Asia?

For any one of those three great apostles, if we looked at the beginning of the story, we'd never believe the end of it. But we know the end of it now. We know how all three died martyrs, and we know how all three left permanent legacies that we, their Christian daughters and sons nearly two millennia later, treasure as our most precious inheritance.

And surely the very unlikelihood of Jesus' choices has its purpose. Peter the denier, Paul the hothead, Thomas the doubter — they all fulfilled their missions in spite of their doubts and disabilities. Peculiar choices though they were, they founded a Church that has lasted two thousand years.

So what's our excuse?

If Peter, who could never make up his mind and was always embarrassing himself by rushing into things without thinking, could lead the Church when it was youngest and most vulnerable, couldn't we at least get to Mass on Sunday?

If Paul, the hothead who got into shouting matches with Peter, could write the most profound meditation on love that ever flowed out of a pen, couldn't we at least be a little more charitable? a little less gossipy? a trifle less wrathful or cruel? a lot more forgiving?

If Thomas, who doubted the resurrection and was too sick to travel, could found a church that endured two thousand years of interesting times in isolation from the rest of Christianity, couldn't we at least ask for his help in overcoming our own doubts?

The apostles are our models and inspirations, not because they're perfect Christians, but because they're so wonderfully imperfect. If Jesus had chosen his disciples from the top half-percent of the virtuous faithful, the rest of us would have no hope at all. But Jesus chose very ordinary men with very ordinary weaknesses, and gave them the grace to carry on in spite of those weaknesses.

That's what gives us hope. Peter, Paul, and Thomas weren't naturally any better than we are. They grew into great founders of our Church because they took the help Christ gave them, not because they had it in them to begin with. If they can do their part, then we can do our part.

And of all the apostles, Thomas may be the one who speaks most to our skeptical age. It's no accident that neo-Gnostics and anti-Christians have tried to make him their spokesman. Ours is an age of doubt, and Thomas is the doubter we remember.

But Thomas isn't leading us to doubt. Remember that doubt is *not* the destination; it's the *route*. Doubt is how we come to certainty. Thomas is waiting to lead us *through* our doubt into certainty — if we'll follow him the whole way.

Prayer

O glorious St. Thomas: When your hand touched Jesus' side, you found the perfection of good things. By your own unbelief and your subsequent faith, you confirm those who are tempted. For you proclaimed to all people how your Lord and your God became incarnate on this earth for us, was nailed to the cross and suffered death, and had a spear open his side, from which we draw life.

By the vision you had of divine things, you became, O Apostle Thomas, the mystic cup of the wisdom of Christ, which gives joy to the souls of the faithful. You were the spiritual net, drawing men from the sea of ignorance. Thus, you came from Zion as a stream of charity, watering the world with the divine dogmas. You imitated the passion of Jesus. You were pierced in your side. You have put on immortality.

Pray to God, to have mercy on our souls. Amen.

— Adapted from Greek liturgical prayers
(See *The Liturgical Year* by Dom Prosper Guéranger,
Prayers for December 21.)

APPENDIX A: THE INDIAN TRADITION

The Indian tradition of St. Thomas is preserved in the hearts of the people who proudly call themselves "Thomas Christians." They tell the story over and over, traditionally at weddings and celebrations. It is the story of how they came to be who they are.

Two of the traditional Thomas sagas were written down shortly after the Portuguese arrived in India. One of them, the "Song of Thomas Ramban," is a kind of chronicle, giving the whole story of Thomas; the other, the "Way-Dance Song" (or Margam Kali), is a series of stanzas that give vivid descriptions of individual incidents. The poems supplement each other, and where they coincide they tell the same incidents in the same order.

From these traditional sources, we have built a complete narration of the career of Thomas in India, the way the Indian Christians have been telling the story for centuries.

No temple on earth was ever so glorious as Solomon's. Its fame reached even India, and King Cholan, having heard of it, decided he must have a palace like it in his own country.

So the king sent for his trusted servant Avan. "You must go," he said, "to the land flowing with milk and honey: a land that thrives above all others, so that it might truly be called the abode of God. It is a western land that stretches from the north to the south. There you shall go and find a carpenter. Take plenty of wealth with you, so that all who see may wonder and be pleased."

The king gave Avan a large sum of gold and sent him on his way. Avan gathered together all the provisions he would need for the long journey.

"O God," he prayed, "you who hold sea and land in your hand, you are my help. Sea of mercy, from the sea take me to the land and help me in my mission."

Having given praise to God, he embarked on his journey by the most direct route, and neither wind nor storm opposed him.

When he landed, he asked directions, and found guides to take him to Mahosa.

While they were wandering the streets in Mahosa, the Lord appeared to them and asked them where they had come from, who they were, and what they had with them.

They showed him the wealth they had brought. "We have come by command of King Cholan to find a good carpenter for fine and faultless work," they told him. "But tell us, how shall we find such a man in a land where we are as lost as if we had no hands and no feet?"

The Lord replied with gracious politeness. "In less than a quarter hour," he told them, "I shall give you a carpenter from this very place. He can do work in wood, stone, gold, silver, copper, iron, and any other kind of work you require, all in the finest manner. There is no better carpenter in the world, and no work that can equal his in beauty or grandeur."

Even as the Lord spoke these words, the angels, obeying his will, joyfully came to the Twin. They brought him, dressed as a carpenter, speeding through the sky to the place where the Lord waited. He arrived there before the quarter hour had passed.

When Avan saw him walking toward the Lord, he was delighted, for Thomas looked every bit the expert carpenter. Seeing Avan's delight, the Lord told him, "Here is your carpenter coming now."

Avan then spoke directly to Thomas, telling him why he had come. But hearing Avan's words, and seeing his strange foreign dress, Thomas broke down and fell weeping at the Lord's feet.

"Until now you have preserved me from every snare," he said. "But now all that counts for nothing. India is full of snakes and wild beasts. They have no books and no good language. The whole country is a forest. O Lord, would you forsake me utterly? Would you toss me into the sea? The people in India are hardly human; they have nothing human in their hearts. They have no religion, not even such as the Gentiles have. They marry dead bodies; they roast their dead like fish. They hate their own children, and their children hate them. O Lord, disciples usually go to other countries in pairs. I cannot understand you! Would you send me away as though I were your enemy? I have no other friends to take away my grief!"

Thus Thomas spoke, with many tears. But the Lord, the Messiah, who shines everywhere, answered him: "Do not suppose that you will be alone. I am with you as your companion wherever you go. And do not be so grieved at being sent to India. They are not beasts there. They will be able to understand your language, and they will hear what you say and understand what you think. Have no fear, but make up your mind and go. I am taking the money for you now, and writing out a receipt."

At these words, Avan handed the money to the Lord, and received his receipt. Then the Lord took the money and gave it to Thomas. With a few more soothing words, he bade him farewell, and Thomas now gladly went with Avan back to his ship. Thus he embarked from Arabia in the year 50 of the Messiah.

On the way the ship stopped at Malyankara. Though the stop was for only eight days, Thomas performed many miracles there, and by the time he left he had established the religion in that city. Then he embarked again, and by the grace of God he at last reached Mylapore, the city of King Cholan.

As soon as Cholan saw him and spoke to him, he knew this was the carpenter he had wished for. Thomas drew a picture of Solomon's temple for Cholan — a picture so exquisite in detail, and so magnificently executed, that it gladdened the hearts of all who saw it. Now Cholan was certain that Thomas was the right architect to build his palace.

Thomas and Cholan conversed for a long time. Thomas made arrangements to collect money as needed to pay for wood and the best stone. "Do not worry too much about the money," he told Cholan. "In a year at the latest, I shall return here, and I shall bring all the tools necessary for the work."

When they heard all Thomas had to say, Cholan and his ministers were very well pleased. They joined together and gave thanks to God for sending them Thomas.

Having made all his arrangements, Thomas went his way, preaching the religion of grace, and spending all the money he had collected for the benefit of the poor and the sick. In a while he passed out of Cholan's country and took part in the marriage feast of Paul's daughter.

But there were some of the heathens who were incensed at the farewell blessing he gave. One of them slapped Thomas on the cheek; and straightaway a tiger bit off the hand that had slapped him. Later that day a dog came back into the hall carrying the hand in its mouth.

When they heard what had happened, Paul and the people of his land believed the faith that Thomas preached. They were all baptized; then they all went together with Thomas and found the hand, and Thomas healed the man who had slapped him, so that his hand was whole again.

From there Thomas wandered as far as China; but in a while he retuned to Mylapore. In order that he might be seen to keep his promise, he worked on the palace for a while. King Cholan gave him more money for the work, but once again Thomas spent it all for the benefit of the poor.

After a year, Thomas set out again, this time for the Kerala country, reaching Malyankara in December of the year 51 of the Messiah. In the year and a half that he spent there, the king, his family, and three thousand other heathens were baptized, as well as forty Jews who had settled in the country. He built a church there and set up a cross, so that they might bow down to it every day. He consecrated Keppa, the nephew of the reigning king, as a bishop, and ordained two priests to spread the faith. Then, with Keppa as his companion, he went toward the southern country.

From village to village he went, everywhere setting up crosses and baptizing thousands of new believers. He ordained priests, established the liturgy, and taught the new believers all they needed to know about the religion of grace.

At last he came back to the land of King Cholan.

Nine years had gone by since King Cholan commissioned the palace, but there was still no palace to be seen. Cholan's ministers finally persuaded the King to send for Thomas.

When the messengers arrived, Thomas did not hesitate. He immediately set off with them, and they brought him into the presence of King Cholan.

Cholan spoke to him as mildly as he could, not wanting to spoil the work if Thomas indeed had a good report to give. "A long time has gone by, and much gold has been spent on stone and wood. But no one has even seen so much as a trace of a foundation. I am tired of seeing mountains of wood and stone piled up. Everyone who sees them mocks me, saying, 'So this is Cholan's palace!' I wish to see the palace finished before I die. If you have any love for me, show it to me without delay."

When Cholan had finished speaking, Thomas made his reply. "Hear me now, and do not be suspicious or angry. All the gold spent on stone and wood is building you a palace that will most certainly satisfy you when you see it. What a beautiful place it is! Even the doors are set with pearl and diamond. In that place, where the love of God dwells, there are nine stones. For those who reach it the sun never sets. If mortals come there through death, they have no sorrow, but only unspeakable joy. There is a lamp like a jewel there — it puts the sun to shame! And never does it grow dim. For him who enters it, all sorrow is banished, and never again will he fear darkness or fire. Ten roads lead to the palace, and seven stairs go up to the tower."[2]

"I wish to hear more of this," the king replied. "We can speak of it more tomorrow; there will be plenty of

---

[2] Symbolizing ten commandments and seven sacraments.

time. But now let us go at once to look more closely at this house. I do not love you if you say, 'Not today, but tomorrow.' You know that I do most certainly love you and respect you, but that will do you no good if you delay even a quarter hour longer."

Now Thomas knew that the king was not pleased with him. "But though it may destroy our friendship and make the king angry," he said to himself, "I must tell the truth." So he addressed the king with confidence.

"The day for seeing it has not come," Thomas said. "Do not be in a hurry. You may see the palace when you die, and then you can go and live there forever. That is the excellent house that your gold has bought you."

At these words, Cholan was speechless. He stood in a daze, unable to speak for anger. When at last he recovered from his stupor, he roared like a lion. He threw Thomas in prison, and Avan along with him, and ordered that they should be held for execution.

When Thomas and Avan had been led off in chains, Cholan, in great distress, called for his younger brother.

"Come near, my brother, and hear me. No reign has ever been spoiled like mine. No ruler has ever been disgraced as I have been today. I am no longer fit to rule. You must rule in my place, my brother."

The younger brother, who loved the king dearly, was so much distressed by his brother's disgrace that he fell into a sickness. Day by day, by God's providence, the disease grew more serious, until at last the angels took his soul and bore it away to heaven.

There he saw a house with Cholan's name written on it. Seeing the name, he went in, and gazed with wonder at the palace he found. Everything to delight body, mind, and spirit was there. All the sorrows that man is subject to vanished when he entered it. It was a palace fit for the greatest of kings.

Joyfully the angels bore his soul back to earth. They covered his body like a shroud. Suddenly the soul filled the body, and the young prince awoke and stood up in perfect health. He gave praise to the Supreme Life; then, without letting anyone else know, he hastened to his elder brother's presence. There he stood with folded hands.

When he saw his brother standing alive before him, Cholan ran and embraced him with a joy that could not be expressed. The young prince told Cholan all about the palace and the wonders he had seen inside it. The king was filled with desire to see it himself, and begged his brother to tell him everything in detail.

Then, to do justice to Thomas and Avan, the king went with all his attendants in high state to the prison. There, seeing the great sage bound like a criminal, King Cholan fell weeping at his feet and confessed his guilt. Then he himself loosed the bonds, while Thomas stood bending over him.

The whole people watched astonished as Thomas and Avan were placed in the king's own chariot and led away from the prison.

"They are going to the palace," some said.

But others said, "They are being taken to be beaten, whipped, and scourged. Enough of this rogue's architecture! In a moment we shall see him get what he deserves."

All along the way, the spectators talked about the strange sight. "They are being taken away to be killed," some said. "No, not killed, but thrown out of the kingdom," others replied.

But what astonishment there was when Thomas and Avan were led to the palace with all the signs of the greatest love and respect! They were taken straight to the tower and seated. There Thomas, with no sign of resentment at all, preached the religion of grace. And they all understood it: Cholan, his brother, Avan, and the whole multitude. With great reverence and joy, they were all baptized together in the name of the Trinity, and they gladly accepted the faith.

As soon as he could, Thomas set up a cross there for their worship. For two and a half years he preached the religion there, and in that time he baptized seven thousand. At that time Patros and Paulos were kings of Chandrapuri; he consecrated Paulos as bishop, and under him six priests of the religion to govern his flock. The people entrusted all their possessions to Thomas, and he gave them rules for conduct.

But at last it was time for him to move on. First he went by land back to the Malayalam country, pausing at many villages and cities along the way to preach the faith. Wherever he went, he established churches, ordained priests, and gave the people rules for their conduct, and finally gave them the gift of the Holy Spirit. In all his travels his faithful companion Keppa never left his side. At last he came to the hill city of Chayal, where he had preached many years before. There again he built a church, ordained a priest, and gave them all the necessary rules of conduct. He stayed there for a year, and eventually gave them the gift of the Holy Spirit.

In time, however, he decided to go to countries where the knowledge of the faith had not yet come. To his faithful disciple Keppa, who had never parted from him, he gave his own garment. Thomas laid his hand on Keppa's head and entrusted the government of the believers to him, telling them to accept Keppa as they would accept him. In honor of his master, the priest he had ordained gladly took the name Tomma. The priests of that place have been named Tomma ever since. Thomas gave him his blessing; then, seeing that he had all the necessary knowledge, he gave him the title of Rampan. He also gave Tomma a book, as a memorial of St. Thomas' preaching of the Gospel in the Kerala country.

How his friends wept to see him go! The whole congregation was bathed in tears. Keppa and Tomma went with him for seven and a half miles; then, by the help of the angels, Thomas left them and departed for the Pandya country.

Up to that time, Thomas had done many remarkable miracles.

He brought to life 29 dead persons;
he cast out Satan from 260 persons;
he healed 230 lepers;
he gave sight to 230 blind persons;
he made whole the arms and legs of 220
   withered persons;
he cured the weakness of tongue of 20;
he healed about 280 sick persons whom all
   the physicians had given up as hopeless.

He did so much good everywhere he went, on account of the more-than-human virtues shining in him, that he won the souls of 17,480 people. Of these,

6,850 were Brahmans,
2,590 Kshatrias,
3,780 Vaisyas, and
4,280 Sudras.[3]

Such high castes he brought into the religion of grace.

He consecrated two great kings as bishops, and he ordained seven kings, lords of villages, as priests — four of whom, for the prosperity of the faith, he made Rampans. He gave 21 chiefs the management of the common fund. And every other arrangement necessary for the good of the faith he had made. When he left, the dignitaries were conducting all the business of the faith in the proper manner, without in the least infringing the rules he had given them.

---

[3] The figures add up to 17,500.

The jewel-like faith shone brighter every day, and every day more heathens were baptized. The number of heathens who did not accept the faith was visibly diminishing. The religion of grace was spreading throughout the length and breadth of the world.

Seeing this, the Emprans bestirred themselves. Everywhere they looked for Thomas, but they could not find him. They began to grow anxious. They raged against anyone who denied having seen him; they raged against their own friends for not telling them when they had found him.

On the third day of July, in the year 72, St. Thomas, who brought several castes to the Messiah, arrived as a traveler at Chinnamala in Mylapore. He was about to pass by a temple of Kali when the Emprans, who had gathered there that day, saw him.

At once they surrounded him and prepared to take their revenge.

"No one shall pass this way today without worshipping at this shrine," they warned him. "If you will bow down and worship Kali and fall at her feet, we shall give you plenty of porridge. You may eat it and go your way."

"Do you suppose I would worship Satan for a meal of unstewed rice?" Thomas replied. "I will never bow down to Kali. If I did bow down, this whole temple would be destroyed by fire."

These words infuriated the Emprans. "Indeed?" they sneered. "We must see the truth of these contemptuous words!"

Suddenly St. Thomas turned to Kali, gazed intently, and commanded the temple to catch fire. At his order, Satan set the temple ablaze, and Kali fell at St. Thomas' feet.

The crowd began to flee in all directions. Kali herself ran away like a mad dog. The wind fed the fire and spread it with no hindrance. Running for their lives, all the people cursed Kali. Some of the Emprans themselves were caught up in the blaze and burned, doomed to be burned again in the eternal fire.

But one of the men who had been caught in the fire leaped out, and — how can we bear to speak these words? — he thrust a great lance deep into the chest of St. Thomas.

Then all the Emprans fled and hid themselves, every one of them.

St. Thomas, alone in the forest by the sea, fell on a stone and prayed.

Angels carried the news to Bishop Paulos. Bishop Paulos and the Great King and all their attendants came running to the rock close to the shrine of Kali.

Immediately, Bishop Paulos pulled out the lance from the fresh wound. Then he tried to put St. Thomas in his chariot to take him away to be healed.

"No need for healing," St. Thomas said. He was still fully conscious. "My bliss is near."

A crowd had gathered around him. So that they might feel joy instead of sorrow at his suffering, he gave them all blessings.

Until half an hour before sunset, St. Thomas spoke with the two kings, telling them many things. Then, alas, his time had come. His soul, resembling a white dove, ascended to supreme bliss in heaven, accompanied by angels dressed in white. Then the heavenly chorus sang his praises, accompanied by every kind of musical instrument.

The two kings took his glorious body in solemn state and laid it in the church. There they all prayed in worship to gain blessings. In the morning, all returned to the church in sorrow.

Angels brought the news of the death to Bishop Keppa, the faithful disciple. Along with the two Rampans, Malihakka and Katappur, he reached the church on the twenty-first day of July. The two bishops, their priests, and all the people offered many prayers and devotions for ten days, with no break in the ceremonies.

Then St. Thomas granted them a great miracle. On all of them shone a golden light. They saw a heavenly house, more beautiful than anyone could describe. Bishop Paulos said that this was the house he had seen before. All heard heavenly music, so glorious that mortal language cannot describe it.

In the house, on a throne, sat St. Thomas himself in state. He lovingly gave many good words of advice to his people, and many great blessings.

"By me," he said, "good will come to my children who remember my death. I shall do good to all those who worship at my tomb."

After they heard these words, all the sights disappeared, and all the people went away joyfully to their homes.

APPENDIX B: LETTER OF POPE PAUL VI

Sent to Cardinal William Conway on the occasion of the 19th centenary of the martyrdom of St. Thomas the Apostle.

Pope Paul VI, to our Reverend Brother William Conway of the Holy Roman Church, Archbishop of Armagh.

Our Reverend Brother, greetings and Apostolic Blessing.

As ancient tradition planted in our souls reports, Saint Thomas, Apostle of Christ, in the year 72, nineteen centuries ago, poured out his blood for his Master in India, to which place he had carried the message of the Gospel. In the city of Madras in the district called Mylapore, where there stands a famous church well-known for its tomb of the Apostle, celebrations will soon take place for the sake of commemorating him, celebrations which (it is anticipated) will be distinguished by the presence of large numbers of foreign visitors. Moreover, impelled by pastoral solicitude, the authorities in India have decided that these celebrations should be conducted with the aim of promoting piety and with events that cultivate the intellect, rather than with external pomp.

In very truth the name of Thomas the Apostle places before the eyes of the mind the gift of faith, since the Lord said to him, "Blessed are those who have not seen and who have believed" (Jn 20:29). Faith moreover is the basis of everlasting life, by which we are made "participants in the divine nature" (2 Pt 1:4). Tradition says that Thomas carried into India a priceless gift of this kind, received from the Savior; for this reason, the following brief motto has deservedly and fittingly been proposed for the ceremonies mentioned above: "Life, which we desire to share."

Taking advantage of this opportunity which has been presented, our attention is drawn to those faithful people of India who, named after St. Thomas, have preserved throughout so many centuries the Christian observance, feeding the flame, as it were, even in those periods during which they were cut off from the West. We are touched with great joy because they, who keep their ancient and special rite, have in recent times gladly accepted additions to it. But even beyond their places and their traditions Catholicism has grown, especially because of the work of missionaries, among whom many Irish are numbered with praise, in such a way that today the ecclesiastical structure in all of India has a firm foundation; it is sufficient to make mention of this country's own sacred hierarchy and the priestly and religious vocations which are known to flourish there.

Therefore we (who have first-hand knowledge of the Church in India, since we had the opportunity to spend time in that important region on account of the world-wide Eucharistic Congress in Bombay) are eagerly directing our attention to the Madras celebrations. In order to be present at them in some way, we appoint and name you, our Reverend Brother, as our special delegate to represent our person in these same gatherings.

Saint Thomas is said to have died on behalf of that same faith which he had preached. "Martyrs are witnesses of God. God wished to have men as witnesses, in order that men too might have God as a witness." (St. Augustine, *On the Letter of John to the Parthians* 1:2 = Patrologia Latina 35:1979). Witness to universal truth (although without the suffering of cruel punishments) is never impressed on our souls enough, since such witness is powerful in expanding the kingdom of God. The Second

Vatican Ecumenical Council openly proclaimed this: "Let all know that our first and most urgent duty for the spread of the faith is to live the Christian life in a profound way" (*Decree on the Church's Missionary Activity*, 36). Therefore we earnestly desire and ask God that an increased sense of this duty will be one of the wholesome results which we are permitted to hope will arise from the aforementioned celebrations.

Therefore since these things impel our spirit, we bestow our Apostolic Blessing (harbinger of divine graces) with great affection on you, our Reverend Brother; and also on the Cardinals of the Holy Roman Church Valerian Gracias, Archbishop of Bombay, and Joseph Parecattil, Archbishop of Ernakulam; likewise on beloved Archbishop Rayappa Arulappa, Archbishop of Madras and Mylapore; on all the other clergy in India; and on all who will participate in these celebrations.

— Given at Rome, at Saint Peter's, on the 18th day of
March, in the year 1972
(the ninth of our Pontificate)

APPENDIX C: POPE JOHN PAUL II

"Let us also go, that we may die with him" (Jn 11:16).

With these words, Saint Thomas showed his desire to be with Jesus, even in the face of death. At the same time, Saint Thomas spoke these words to the other disciples to inspire in them a similar love for Jesus, to stir up in them the same courage and devotion.

"Let us also go, that we may die with him."

According to tradition, at this very place, which is now called Saint Thomas Mount, the great Apostle of India fulfilled his own exhortation. Out of love for Jesus, here in Madras, Saint Thomas died for Christ. He gave his life as a martyr for the sake of Christ and the Gospel.

Dear friends in Christ, and you especially, dear children: let us ask God for strong faith and courage. Let us love Jesus as Saint Thomas did. Let us offer him our lives day after day, so that we may live with him forever.

— Address in Madras, India, February 5, 1986

On this happy occasion, I am reminded of the words of Jesus: "I am the way, and the truth, and the life" (Jn 14:6). These words were first spoken in reply to a question of Saint Thomas, who had asked: "Lord, how can we know the way?"

As Christians of Kerala, you trace your spiritual heritage to the preaching of this great Apostle. And just as Saint Thomas discovered that Jesus himself is the answer to the question, so you too, together with the whole Church, have come to believe that Jesus is "the way, and the truth, and the life." This revelation by God is the cause of our joy and the foundation of our faith. May we always praise God for the great privilege of knowing Jesus Christ as our Lord and Savior.

— Address in Ernakulam, India, February 8, 1986

Appendix D: Pope Benedict XVI

Audience on St. Thomas.

Thomas the Twin

Dear Brothers and Sisters,

Continuing our encounters with the Twelve Apostles chosen directly by Jesus, today we will focus our attention on Thomas. Ever present in the four lists compiled by the New Testament, in the first three Gospels he is placed next to Matthew (cf. Mt 10:3; Mk 3:18; Lk 6:15), whereas in Acts, he is found after Philip (cf. Acts 1:13).

His name derives from a Hebrew root, *ta'am*, which means "paired, twin". In fact, John's Gospel several times calls him "Dydimus" (cf. Jn 11:16; 20:24; 21:2), a Greek nickname for, precisely, "twin". The reason for this nickname is unclear.

It is above all the Fourth Gospel that gives us information that outlines some important traits of his personality.

The first concerns his exhortation to the other Apostles when Jesus, at a critical moment in his life, decided to go to Bethany to raise

Lazarus, thus coming dangerously close to Jerusalem (Mk 10: 32).

On that occasion Thomas said to his fellow disciples: "Let us also go, that we may die with him" (Jn 11:16). His determination to follow his Master is truly exemplary and offers us a valuable lesson: it reveals his total readiness to stand by Jesus, to the point of identifying his own destiny with that of Jesus and of desiring to share with him the supreme trial of death.

In fact, the most important thing is never to distance oneself from Jesus.

Moreover, when the Gospels use the verb "to follow", it means that where he goes, his disciple must also go.

Thus, Christian life is defined as a life with Jesus Christ, a life to spend together with him. St Paul writes something similar when he assures the Christians of Corinth: "You are in our hearts, to die together and to live together" (II Cor 7: 3). What takes place between the Apostle and his Christians must obviously apply first of all to the relationship between Christians and Jesus himself: dying together, living together, being in his Heart as he is in ours.

A second intervention by Thomas is recorded at the Last Supper. On that occasion, predicting his own imminent departure, Jesus announced that he was going to prepare a place for his disciples so that they could be where he is found; and he explains to them: "Where [I] am going you know the way" (Jn 14:4). It is then that Thomas intervenes, saying: "Lord, we do not know where you are going; how can we know the way?" (Jn 14:5).

In fact, with this remark he places himself at a rather low level of understanding; but his words provide Jesus with the opportunity to pronounce his famous definition: "I am the Way, and the Truth and the Life" (Jn 14:6).

Thus, it is primarily to Thomas that he makes this revelation, but it is valid for all of us and for every age. Every time we hear or read these words, we can stand beside Thomas in spirit and imagine that the Lord is also speaking to us, just as he spoke to him.

At the same time, his question also confers upon us the right, so to speak, to ask Jesus for explanations. We often do not understand him. Let us be brave enough to say: "I do not understand you, Lord; listen to me, help me to understand." In such a way — with this frankness, which is the true way of praying, of speaking to Jesus — we express our meager capacity to understand and at the same time place ourselves in the trusting attitude of someone who expects light and strength from the One able to provide them.

Then, the proverbial scene of the doubting Thomas that occurred eight days after Easter is very well known. At first he did not believe that Jesus had appeared in his absence and said: "Unless I see in his hands the print of the nails, and place my finger in the mark of the nails, and place my hand in his side, I will not believe" (Jn 20:25).

Basically, from these words emerges the conviction that Jesus can now be recognized by his wounds rather than by his face. Thomas holds that the signs that confirm Jesus' identity are now above all his wounds, in which he reveals to us how much he loved us. In this the Apostle is not mistaken.

As we know, Jesus reappeared among his disciples eight days later and this time Thomas was present. Jesus summons him: "Put your finger here, and see my hands; and put out your hand, and place it in my side; do not be faithless, but believing" (Jn 20:27).

Thomas reacts with the most splendid profession of faith in the whole of the New

Testament: "My Lord and my God!" (Jn 20:28). St Augustine comments on this: Thomas "saw and touched the man, and acknowledged the God whom he neither saw nor touched; but by the means of what he saw and touched, he now put far away from him every doubt, and believed the other" (*In ev. Jo.* 121, 5).

The Evangelist continues with Jesus' last words to Thomas: "Have you believed because you have seen me? Blessed are those who have not seen and yet believe" (Jn 20:29). This sentence can also be put into the present: "Blessed are those who do not see and yet believe".

In any case, here Jesus spells out a fundamental principle for Christians who will come after Thomas, hence, for all of us.

It is interesting to note that another Thomas, the great Medieval theologian of Aquinas, juxtaposed this formula of blessedness with the apparently opposite one recorded by Luke: "Blessed are the eyes which see what you see!" (Lk 10:23). However, Aquinas comments: "Those who believe without seeing are more meritorious than those who, seeing, believe" (*In Johann.* XX *lectio* VI 2566).

In fact, the Letter to the Hebrews, recalling the whole series of the ancient biblical Patriarchs who believed in God without seeing the fulfilment of his promises, defines faith as "the assurance of things hoped for, the conviction of things not seen" (Heb 11:1).

The Apostle Thomas' case is important to us for at least three reasons: first, because it comforts us in our insecurity; second, because it shows us that every doubt can lead to an outcome brighter than any uncertainty; and, lastly, because the words that Jesus addressed to him remind us of the true meaning of mature faith and encourage us to persevere, despite the difficulty, along our journey of adhesion to him.

A final point concerning Thomas is preserved for us in the Fourth Gospel, which presents him as a witness of the Risen One in the subsequent event of the miraculous catch in the Sea of Tiberias (cf. Jn 21:2ff.).

On that occasion, Thomas is even mentioned immediately after Simon Peter: an evident sign of the considerable importance that he enjoyed in the context of the early Christian communities.

Indeed, the *Acts* and the *Gospel of Thomas*, both apocryphal works but in any case important for the study of Christian origins, were written in his name.

Lastly, let us remember that an ancient tradition claims that Thomas first evangelized Syria and Persia (mentioned by Origen, according to Eusebius of Caesarea, *Ecclesiastical History* 3, 1) then went on to Western India (cf. *Acts of Thomas* 1-2 and 17ff.), from where also he finally reached Southern India.

Let us end our reflection in this missionary perspective, expressing the hope that Thomas' example will never fail to strengthen our faith in Jesus Christ, Our Lord and Our God.

— Given in Rome, September 27, 2006

ACKNOWLEDGMENTS

We wish to thank all those who prayed this work into publication — St. Thomas first and foremost, but also (a close second) Father Thomas Acklin, OSB, who encouraged us for a decade to persevere with our research and writing. His brother Benedictines at Asirvanam Monastery in Bangalore helped us to locate rare Indian volumes, as did Father Emmanuel Kaniamparampil, OCD, Gaurav Shroff, Dr. George Menachery, and the folks at Merging Currents Books (Bangalore). The classicist Michael Gilleland assisted us in translating Pope Paul VI's letter on St. Thomas from its original Latin. (All other papal material is from the official translations on the Vatican's Web site.) Kevin Edgecomb led us to Thomas-related material in the Eastern liturgies. Historian Adrian Murdoch kept us informed about archeological digs related to India's trade with Rome. Father Jose Uppani gave us needed encouragement as we brought the work to a conclusion.

We, of course, bear sole responsibility for any mistakes made in spite of the best efforts of these good people.

— The Authors
Feast of St. Thomas the Apostle, 2009

WORKS CONSULTED

Anthonysamy, S. J. *A Saga of Faith: St. Thomas the Apostle of India.* Chennai (India): Santhome Cathedral Basilica, 2004.

Casson, Lionel. *The Ancient Mariners.* Princeton: Princeton University Press, 1991.

Goodspeed, Edgar. *The Twelve: The Story of Christ's Apostles.* Philadelphia: Winston, 1957.

Grant, Michael. *The Jews in the Roman World.* London: Phoenix, 1999.

Green, Peter. *Alexander of Macedon, 356-323 B.C.* Berkeley and Los Angeles: University of California Press, 1991.

Huddleston, Fr. Trevor. *Christian India.* London and New York: Thames and Hudson, 1957.

Jenkins, Philip. *Hidden Gospels: How the Search for Jesus Lost Its Way.* Oxford: Oxford University Press, 2001.

Kaniarakath, George, CMI. *Person and Faith of Apostle Thomas in the Gospels.* New Delhi: Intercultural Publications, 2000.

Katz, Nathan. *Who Are the Jews of India?* Berkeley and Los Angeles: University of California Press, 2000.

Klijn, A. F. J. *The Acts of Thomas: Introduction, Text, and Commentary.* Leiden, Netherlands: Brill, 2003.

Kollamparampil, Antony George. *From Symbol to Truth: A Syriac Understanding of the Paschal Mystery.* Rome: Edizioni Liturgiche, 2000.

Kurikilamkatt, James. *First Voyage of the Apostle Thomas to India: Ancient Christianity in Bharuch and Taxila.* Bangalore: Asian Trading Corporation, 2005.

McBirnie, William Steuart. *The Search for the Twelve Apostles.* Wheaton, IL: Tyndale House, 1973.

McDermott, Rachel Fell, and Jeffrey J. Kripal (editors). *Encountering Kali.* Berkeley and Los Angeles: University of California Press, 2003.

Menachery, George (editor). *The Nazranies.* Thiruvananthapuram, India: South Asia Research Assistance Services, 1998. (This is a single-volume compilation of the full text of fifteen academic books and twenty-two shorter scholarly studies of St. Thomas, all published in the nineteenth and twentieth centuries.)

————. *The Thomapedia.* Thiruvananthapuram, India: St. Joseph's Press, 2000.

Most, Glenn W. *Doubting Thomas.* Cambridge, MA: Harvard University Press, 2005.

Mundadan, A. M. *History of Christianity in India.* Bangalore: CHAI, 2001.

Palatty, Paul. *Thomas in the Fourth Gospel.* Alwaye, Kerala, India: St. Thomas Academy for Research, 2001.

Patai, Raphael. *The Children of Noah: Jewish Seafaring in Ancient Times.* Princeton: Princeton University Press, 1998.

Puthur, Bosco (editor). *St. Thomas Christians and Nambudiris Jews and Sangam Literature.* Kochi, Kerala, India: L.R.C. Publications, 2003.

Robertson, Ronald, CSP. *The Eastern Christian Churches.* Rome: Edizione Orientalia Christiana, 1999.

Ruffin, C. Bernard. *The Twelve: The Lives of the Apostles after Calvary.* Huntington, IN: Our Sunday Visitor, 1998.

Thapar, Romila. *A History of India, Vol. 1.* Baltimore: Penguin Books, 1966.

Vadakkekara, Benedict. *Origin of India's St. Thomas Christians: A Historiographical Critique.* Delhi: Media House, 1995.

VanderKam, James C. *An Introduction to Early Judaism.* Grand Rapids, MI, and Cambridge, England: William B. Eerdmans Publishing Company, 2001.

Wylen, Stephen M. *The Jews in the Time of Jesus.* Mahwah, NJ: Paulist Press, 1996.